ROME

AUTHENTIC RECIPES CELEBRATING THE FOODS OF THE WORLD

Recipes and Text
MAUREEN B. FANT

Photographs
JEAN-BLAISE HALL

General Editor
CHUCK WILLIAMS

BONNIER
BOOKS

CONTENTS

RECIPES

ANTIPASTI

PRIMI

SECONDI

CONTORNI

DOLCI

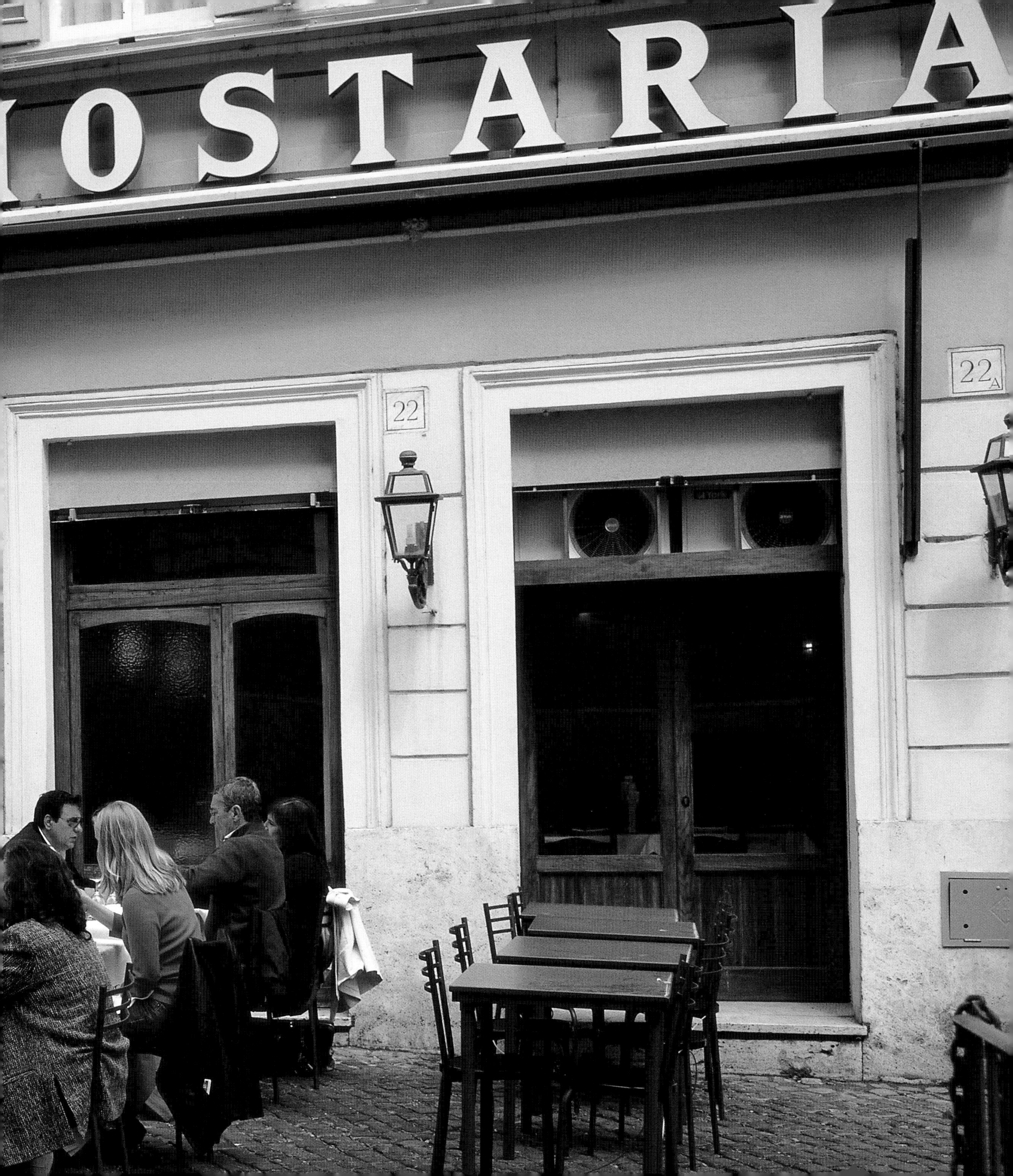
OSTARIA
22
22A

INTRODUCTION

The best Roman food tastes like what it is. Artichokes taste like artichokes, lamb like lamb. Herbs are freshly cut and are usually limited to just one variety per dish. Sometimes the eloquence of this simplicity is lost on visitors, but *la cucina romana* rewards those who take the time to get to know it.

CULINARY HISTORY

The arrival of the tomato and potato from the New World in the sixteenth century did not have a dramatic effect on the Roman diet, despite the wonderful things that local cooks would learn to do with them. Centuries ago, as it is today, the core of the Roman menu was olives and olive oil, pulses, cured pork, lamb, offal, garden-fresh vegetables and wild greens, sheep's milk cheeses and other dairy products, chewy bread baked in wood-burning ovens, pasta, fresh fish, and salted anchovies. Drinks have been equally consistent over time, with local wine and spring water accompanying meals.

At the start of the first millennium BC, Rome, today the focal point of the Lazio (Latium) region, was little more than a river, some uninhabited hills, and a handful of shepherds' huts. Within less than a thousand years, there was a thriving city, a culture, sophisticated systems of transportation and communications, and domination of the Western world. Bread in the capital was baked with grain from North Africa, and dates came from Syria. The food distribution was

analogous to that of Victorian and Edwardian England or the contemporary global trade network. But even during the height of the Roman Empire, there were always statesmen and writers to lament the good old days when a bowl of warm spelt was all the luxury a good Roman needed. Some of the complaining took the form of satirical or hyperbolic accounts of contemporary excess, often with a political agenda. Petronius's first-century AD fictional account of the newly rich Trimalchio's vulgar and extravagant banquet ensured that future generations would think of Roman food as based on a diet of larks' tongues and dormice.

With the fall of the empire, Rome entered a period of isolation and under-population. Roman popular cooking from the sixth to the nineteenth century can be viewed nearly as a whole. The elaborate water distribution system of the ancients was out of commission from the sixth century to the papacy of Nicholas V (1447–55), and the population shrank significantly, with fewer than fifty thousand souls rattling around within walls built for a city of one million. During the Middle Ages,

residents huddled near the Tiber, the principal source of water. They occupied and sometimes destroyed the ancient monuments, and created the architectural imprint that the heart of old Rome still bears today.

The face of Rome changed dramatically after it became the capital of the Kingdom of Italy in 1870, not least because of a sharp increase in population. But until then gardens within the walls, irrigated by canals and streams, provided city dwellers with celery, artichokes, cabbages, chard, and other vegetables. Until the nineteenth century, mills floated on the Tiber and used the river's hydraulic power to grind flour for bread and home-made pasta. Egg pasta was for the rich; the poor made their dough with only flour and water. The usual sauce was often a mixture of pork fat and pecorino until the tomato gained culinary acceptance in the eighteenth century. Dried industrial pasta did not arrive until the late nineteenth century.

Romans went outside the walls to pick the wild chicories and lettuces that covered the countryside. Porcini and *ovoli*, mushrooms

that nowadays command high prices, grew plentifully and were an important part of the popular kitchen.

The city's earliest restaurants were the ancestors of today's wine bar and *tavola calda* (literally, "hot table", a place to get a cheap, hot meal). Examples of the *thermopolium* (hot shop) preserved in Pompeii and in the ancient port, Ostia Antica, show how earthenware jars were embedded in the shop's counter, while wall paintings show the menu of onions, olives, and cheese.

Although for much of its history Rome drew visitors from all parts of the known world, mass tourism began with the medieval Christian pilgrimages, particularly the jubilee year of 1300. For centuries, pilgrims ate at taverns and *osterie,* all of which had names that could be easily depicted in symbols for illiterate patrons (The Falcon, The Two Swords, and so on). Each served a speciality, such as pot roast or slow-cooked pork, and carafes of wine, some of it from vineyards within the city walls. Northern Europeans

on the Grand Tour in the eighteenth and nineteenth centuries enjoyed picturesque *osterie* that were not unlike their predecessors.

The economic boom that followed World War II brought changes both in demography and at the table. While tourists threw their coins in the Trevi Fountain and American movie stars went to work at Cinecittà (dubbed Hollywood-on-the-Tiber), workers from southern Italy introduced new regional culinary influences, such as pizza, to the capital.

In those days, affluence continued to mean calories, of which Ristorante Alfredo's signature *fettuccine al triplo burro* (fettuccine with triple butter, more commonly known as fettuccine Alfredo, and still very popular), can stand as emblematic. Cream sauces trickled down to the trattoria menu as well and weren't uprooted until the days of the post-1968 countercultural eateries, the so-called alternative restaurants. They specialised in dishes that rebelled against tradition, such as salads with canned sweetcorn, whose main virtues were probably ease of preparation

and a total departure from Roman tradition. Fortunately, all the while, a decent *spaghetti alla carbonara* could still be found at any number of neighbourhood trattorias.

By the late 1980s, talented chefs with professional training began using the finest ingredients available to offer original dishes to a more sophisticated clientele. *Cucina creativa,* which was Italy's answer to nouvelle cuisine, established itself in Rome in a handful of very good, very expensive restaurants. Meanwhile, in a somewhat related movement, traditional Roman food (and regional food in general) was being rediscovered and lightened up. After the opening of Rome's first McDonald's in the Piazza di Spagna in 1985, traditionalists went to the barricades. Soon the old-school dishes like *pasta alla gricia* (with bacon, garlic, and chilli), almost forgotten, became the foodies' shibboleth. Around this time the Slow Food Association, based in Piedmont, and the influential *Gambero Rosso* magazine began to raise the profile of both traditional and innovative cooking.

CONTEMPORARY CUISINE

Located almost in the geographic centre of Italy, and for millennia a magnet for pilgrims and visitors, Rome might well have become the gastronomic world in microcosm. Although restaurants that feature creative dishes or imported ingredients are on the rise, Roman menus remain surprisingly loyal to local tradition.

There may be a cell phone on the table, but the main influence on Roman eating is still tradition. Indeed, it sometimes seems that the newer the restaurant, the older the menu, with chefs now doing historical research and chatting with their grandmothers when it comes time to develop recipes.

Cooking in Rome remains ingredient driven, and choices are strictly seasonal. Pasta is the pillar of the cuisine, surrounded by extraordinary vegetables and good, simply cooked meat and fish. Most dishes have only a few elements and fewer secrets: If it is there, you can usually taste it and identify it. Innovation can mean adding one additional ingredient to *spaghetti alla carbonara*.

This doesn't mean that all Romans eat in a museum, of course. Some brilliant and creative chefs are pushing the boundaries. It's just that most people like what they've always eaten, and with good reason. They like looking forward to broad beans in May, figs in June, peaches in July, and persimmons in October. Bankers and bus drivers alike are happy on Thursday mornings because they know their favourite trattoria will be serving gnocchi for lunch. On Tuesdays and Fridays, it's fish. At Christmas and Easter, Romans still give one another gifts of home-baked biscuits. How much longer modern life (complete with encroaching supermarkets and shrinking lunch hours) will allow the status quo to survive is of great concern to many.

Although not immune to food fashion or fad, in general Rome is blissfully free of the sort of fanaticism that eliminates entire food groups from the diet. If you discount six espressos a day and a weakness for pastry and deep-frying – and salami and pancetta – the Roman diet fits the Mediterranean ideal: plenty of fruits and vegetables, lots of pulses, fresh fish, and small amounts of meat, little of it red. The main fat used is olive oil. Delicate Roman gelato makes favourite brands outside Italy seem too dense and rich in comparison. Wine is preferred to spirits, and the tap water is excellent.

Few vegetarian restaurants exist: if you can have *carciofi alla romana* (page 159) for your main course in an ordinary trattoria, what's the point? However, shops that offer *biologico* (organic) food are thriving, and even macrobiotic eating has its fans. Dishes that began to enter the Roman consciousness through the vegetarian-organic back door in the 1990s, such as houmous and tabbouleh, are standards among young people and at the occasional casual party.

Some outside influences maintain a culinary presence in Rome, of which the most venerable are dishes from other regions of Italy. Even a restaurant in Rome that serves *ribollita*, the vegetable soup on every Florentine menu, or *seadas,* the classic Sardinian honey-drenched, cheese-filled fried pastry, is considered exotic.

You'll find almost no French restaurants in Rome, but you may come across a thriving *birreria* (beer hall) offering German sausages, *crauti* (sauerkraut), and, of course, an array of beers. Truly foreign restaurants used to be isolated phenomena. For years, a lone Hungarian restaurant stood alongside the Forum of Trajan, but it became Chinese, and several owners later is now Sicilian, a favourite gastronomic ethnicity (a much more labour-intensive and richly textured cuisine than the Roman). Yet no more than a few Sicilian restaurants are found in the capital.

There are certainly more curry houses than in the past, and Chinese restaurants have proliferated, but unfortunately much of the food served in them is frozen or canned. Most of the few Eritrean and Middle Eastern places mainly attract new foreign residents and the occasional curious Roman seeking a change of pace from familiar regional fare.

The concept of fusion cooking has not really arrived in Rome. Most mixing is limited to the combining of regional specialities.

Well-considered departures from tradition are instead called *cucina creativa*. A chef like Heinz Beck of La Pergola (Rome's only Michelin two-star restaurant), at the Cavalieri Hilton Hotel atop Monte Mario, or Angelo Troiani of Il Convivio, near Piazza Navona, may let their formidable fantasies run freely – they may even use foreign ingredients – but if you read the whole of any given menu, you'll know what time of year it is, where you are, and that the menu was not composed by a committee. Beck's signature is a multiplicity of little dishes, such as artichokes five ways. Troiani is well known for his unusual and enticing combinations: imagine sweet prawns with a touch of bitter Campari.

A trip through the aisles of a Roman supermarket reveals a world of canned sauces and frozen pasta that will quickly dash the illusions of any visitor who imagines happy Italian families tucking into mamma's cooking every day and twice on Sunday. The fact is that some modern Italians are embracing convenience in the form of canned, frozen,

and packet foods. But even harried parents who gratefully accept a time- or energy-saving innovation wherever they find it, or a single person who takes home a juicy spit-roasted chicken from the corner *rosticceria* rather than face the kitchen in solitude, usually know how to cook a decent meal in a pinch. The advice of a mother, an uncle, or a friend is, after all, only a phone call away.

Many people do, of course, love to cook and will gladly spend hours preparing a special dinner for friends, turning out every-thing from scratch. That is the moment to share one's discoveries and gastronomic treasures: the best *mozzarella di bufala* in the capital, a single-vineyard Amarone wine that has been saved for the right Gorgonzola, or a spit-roasted leg of lamb from Abruzzo, just big enough for four. Indeed, some of the best food in Rome can be found in modest home kitchens, where Romans make simple but flavourful meals using many of the same local ingredients their ancestors did in centuries past.

EATING OUT

Rome boasts its share of exclusive Michelin-starred restaurants, but the place to eat out is the trattoria, the casual neighbourhood restaurant serving simple, traditional local food. It used to be the place to go for food just like you ate at home. Today, a trattoria is where you find hearty and authentic regional dishes.

The small, family-run restaurant, whether serving spaghetti or more creative delicacies, provides the most satisfying eating out experiences in Rome. The best-loved places tend to be small, and the owner is present, either in the dining room or the kitchen. And though many people try all the new spots in their search for gastronomic thrills, most return again and again to a couple of favourite places in their own neighbourhood.

When Romans go out to eat, the main appeal may not be the food, but rather the chance to *stare insieme* – to be together with their friends, with someone else doing the work. They'll often order the foods they know, especially those that are too difficult or time-consuming to make at home. There remains a strongly traditional current in Roman dining habits and restaurant menus, with the same dishes continually reappearing. But only lazy cooks make a boring meal – even Sophocles, Euripides, and Shakespeare retold old stories, making them richer and more interesting along the way. As awareness of wines, top ingredients, and artisanal foods from around Italy continues to grow, even some stalwart trattoria menus have become more interesting and sophisticated.

Hallmarks of the Roman table

The day starts early with a coffee and pastry at *il bar*. In Rome, the bar is a coffee stop and gathering place – not just a place to drink

alcohol. The next trip to the bar, for a break or quick lunch, could involve a *tramezzino, pizzetta,* or *medaglione* – each one a different kind of snack or sandwich. At lunch or dinner, restaurants and trattorias offer unhurried meals of two to four courses. A long dinner with plenty of wine and talk is typically the night's entertainment. Many wine bars (page 54) offer meals that tend to be lighter than those from traditional restaurants and are a good choice in the evening, especially if you've had a large lunch.

Romans are not generally known for their polished manners, and waiters are often rude or brusque. The lack of attention to service puts some foreign visitors off, but they should not take it personally – it's just the local way. What the waiters lack in charm, they usually make up for in skill. And if there were no other reason to learn some Italian, it would be worth it to be able to question your waiter about the menu, what the table next to you is having, the size of the clams, and what bottle of wine would go well with your meal.

Attention to décor has come late to the Roman restaurant scene and is not an effective indicator of price and quality. Some of the finest places are at best nondescript: what passes for décor might be a homely accretion of framed pictures and other memorabilia. Some restaurants, however, are particularly known for their good looks. At La Terrazza, in the Hotel Eden, near Via Veneto, picture

windows mean the beautiful view of Rome's rooftops outshines the rest of the room. In the summer, La Pergola sets their tables on the terrace to exploit its extraordinary panorama; in winter the dining room, with plenty of polished wood and brass, and fresh flowers, is no less welcoming. Likewise, restaurant Vecchia Roma's ornate rooms are used most often in winter. In summer, the picturesque Piazza Campitelli, where Vecchia Roma is located, provides possibly the most charming ambience in town. Studied minimalism, as at the 'Gusto wine bar and restaurant, is making inroads in baroque Rome.

Restaurants setting standards

Some of the top restaurants in Rome continue a tradition that has lasted generations and, in some cases, centuries. When the French essayist Montaigne visited Rome in 1580, he stopped at a combination inn and tavern between the Tiber and Piazza Navona called L'Orso (The Bear). And when the celebrated Milanese chef-restaurateur

Gualtiero Marchesi opened his elegant outpost in the capital in 2001 in the same location, he kept the name Hostaria dell'Orso (Inn of the Bear). The venerable Ristorante La Campana, not far away in a street of the same name, has been there since at least the early 1500s. The Hostaria dell'Orso has a piano bar and serves a highly refined creative and classic menu. La Campana is beloved for its trattoria-style *spaghetti all'amatriciana, carciofi alla romana*, and other Roman staples.

Downriver in Testaccio, at Checchino dal 1887, the Mariani siblings serve affluent diners the *quinto quarto* (offal) dishes (page 143) that their great-grandmother made for the abbatoir workers from across the road in the nineteenth century. At Al Presidente, a few steps from the Trevi Fountain, Sebastiano Allegrini serves raw fish "Mediterranean sushi" and a number of traditional fish and meat dishes in the same space his parents once ran a trattoria. Creative chef Agata Parisella, with her husband, Romeo Caraccio, transformed her family's trattoria into the

elegant Ristorante Agata e Romeo, near the church of Santa Maria Maggiore. Massimo Riccioli turned his father's place near the Pantheon, in Via della Rosetta, into the top seafood restaurant in Rome, La Rosetta.

The neighbourhood restaurants of Rome, collectively and loosely grouped under the term "trattoria", cover a very broad range of cuisines and degrees of elegance. Lucia and Augusto, two trattorias in Trastevere, represent the old style – with simple rooms and simpler menus. The *primi* offerings will usually include *pasta alla carbonara* and/or *amatriciana*, while *secondi* are commonly simple grilled meats. Such places are often frequented by tourists seeking the real Rome and Romans seeking familiar fare at a good price. Enoteca Corsi, in Via del Gesù, evolved from the back room of a wine shop. La Piazzetta, near Via Cavour, boasts an updated menu and great desserts. Colline Emiliane, near Piazza Barberini, and La Gensola, in Trastevere, offering Emilian and Sicilian dishes, respectively, are among the few regional trattorias.

MARKETS

The large municipal markets and the small, specialised food shops surrounding them are quite simply the best places to buy ingredients – and to get a recipe, catch up on neighbourhood gossip, have a lesson on the correct use of six kinds of tomatoes, and learn the right way to cut *puntarelle* and *carciofi.*

Shopping for food in Rome's local markets is a skill that foreign residents and visitors would be wise to learn quickly and well. You need to know how to insist on the best quality and how to assert your place in the "queue": It is assumed that if you are not jostling, you are just looking. Visitors with no local kitchen in which to cook their purchases need not miss the experience. Armed with a few key words, they can acquire an excellent picnic to enjoy in one of the city's many parks.

In Rome you don't make a shopping list. You begin to plan your meal when you see what looks best at the market. Depending on the season, you'll find fresh peas and broad beans ready podded, *puntarelle* (Catalonian chicory) skilfully cut, Borettana onions (small, round, and flat) peeled and ready to cook *in agrodolce,* and all the leafy greens – spinach, cavolo nero and various chicories – divested of their tough stalks.

Every quarter of Rome has one large and a number of small markets, most of them open six mornings a week, Monday through Saturday. The most famous central markets are those in Piazza Testaccio and Piazza Campo de' Fiori, and the one near Piazza Vittorio Emanuele. Tucked here and there are miniature versions serving residents of the immediate neighbourhood. Look for one close to the Trevi Fountain in front of the restaurant Al Presidente, in Via Bocca de Leone, near the Piazza di Spagna, and the charming market near the church of San Saba, in the Aventino area.

Not much difference exists between a market stall and a standard small corner shop except for the hours (the shop reopens in the afternoon) and the presence of walls. The most colourful shops are single purpose but broadly interpreted. The *salumeria* or *salsamenteria* sells prosciutto, salamis, and cheeses. The *fruttivendolo* is a greengrocer. The *pescheria* sells fish, and the *macelleria* sells meat. An *alimentari* is a general food shop that does not stock fruit and vegetables.

Campo de' Fiori

The open-air stalls in Campo de' Fiori form the main market of the Centro Storico. Its often photographed array of flowers for sale seems to console the imposing central statue of Giordano Bruno, the philosopher-monk burned at the stake here in 1600. The large, rectangular piazza is located between the beautiful Piazza Farnese, where the French Embassy occupies a magnificent Renaissance palazzo (Palazzo Farnese), and the small piazza that contains the Palazzo della Cancelleria. Around the three piazzas, and along the narrow streets that surround them, are many popular trattorias, bars, and miscellaneous restaurants aimed at tourists and young people, as well as actual residents of this once working-class neighbourhood, now a fashionable address.

It's not the fault of the stall-holders, who are as real as any you'll find in the city, but rather of geography that Campo de' Fiori is the market that draws the most tourists. If you can manage the crowds, you'll find the quality and variety of the produce here are first rate. Look for the large stall of Claudio Zampa in the middle of the piazza. He sells a wide range of the best that is in season and even some exotic fruits. A few fish stalls grouped in one corner sell excellent sea bass, fresh anchovies, and other local favourites.

At another corner of the piazza, close to Piazza Farnese, is one of the best-loved bakeries in all of Rome, Antico Forno del Campo de' Fiori. Sample the *pizza bianca* (page 48), plain or filled with any number of toppings. They also bake a fine *torta di mele* (apple cake), a little-known Roman tradition.

Piazza Vittorio

One of the only places in Rome where you begin to wonder if you're still in Italy is the labyrinthine indoor market between Via Filippo Turati and Via Lamarmora, just south of the Termini station. This is the Esquilino neighbourhood, named for one of Rome's canonical seven hills, and for the past few decades, this is where Rome's growing population of immigrants from Africa, Asia, and the Middle East have come to settle. In the spacious sky-lit market of Piazza Vittorio, you'll have no trouble buying halal meat, green beans from Morocco, dried fish from Bangladesh, and every kind of spice, rice, and pulse. In addition you'll find every sort of local fruit and vegetable, as well as fresh Mediterranean fish and plenty of fresh meats to choose from.

Piazza Testaccio

The heart of the food-oriented Testaccio quarter is the big square market – roofed but open – of Piazza Testaccio. Nearly a whole side of the square is devoted to fishmongers, such as Rosa and Nello, first in the line, who will fillet your fresh anchovies or skin your moray eel while you buy your fruit. Near the fish stalls is the tomato man: here you'll find the finest array of tomatoes in the market, from fleshy Ligurian Cuore di Bue tomatoes to tiny Sicilian Datteri, roughly the size and shape of dates. On the far side of the market are the stall-holders who grow or gather their own produce (the others buy from the whole-sale markets). Check here for wild chicory or for the freshest carrots. The customers are fairly well heeled, but the atmosphere is genuine: There is plenty of good-natured yelling, chatter, and joking among the stall-holders, who can trim artichokes, *puntarelle,* and *broccoletti* like no one else in the city.

Meat is still an important fixture in this neighbourhood, where the old abbatoir was located and all its workers lived and ate. Meats of all kinds are well represented in the market and shops around the square. Food-lovers from all over come to this area just to visit the nearby Volpetti shop in Via Marmorata. Here you will find a store jam-packed with the finest cured meats, fresh and mature cheeses, and condiments from every corner of Italy and beyond.

FLAVOURS OF THE NEIGHBOURHOODS

If every neighbourhood in Rome is well supplied with restaurants, trattorias, *gelaterie,* and coffee bars, as well as places to buy superb greens, *mozzarella di bufala,* and *prosciutto di Parma,* what makes them all so different? It must be the history.

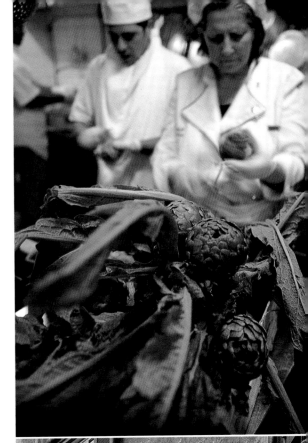

In the first century AD, as part of his plan for remaking the city of Rome, the emperor Augustus divided it into fourteen districts. Today, after two millennia, the city is still made up of districts, or *rioni,* which now number twenty-two within the city's walls (outside are quarters, suburbs, and zones). Many *rioni* preserve a particular urban personality, a combination of the history, architecture, monuments, amenities, and, of course, residents of the area. And though neighbourhood shops provide all the essentials for those living nearby, the finest local shops and restaurants entice people from around the city and around the world.

Trastevere

The name Trastevere means "across the Tiber", and refers to the area on the west bank, south of the river's bend, opposite the Campo Marzio and Testaccio. The *trasteverini* like to call themselves the last true Romans, and they celebrate their identity each summer with the Festa de' Noantri ("the rest of us", meaning the *trasteverini* themselves), held in July. But the densely populated Trastevere district, Rione XIII, is also overflowing with artists, foreign residents, and visitors from less lively neighbourhoods. It is home to the city's only English-language cinema and to one of Rome's oldest churches, beautiful Santa Maria in Trastevere (look for stunning mosaics inside). At night, the areas around Santa Maria and the nearby church of Santa Cecilia, with their small ivy-hung palazzi and narrow,

winding streets, bustle with a kind of post-millennial dolce vita atmosphere. Young people of all stripes and piercings come here to eat, drink, and socialise with each other, which has made living in this once tranquil area something of a challenge.

Trastevere is arguably Rome's most food-laden neighbourhood. Within steps of Piazza San Cosimato, with its open-air market, are shops selling coffee beans and exotic spices, notably Filippetti, in Via Natale del Grande. Tubs of superb ricotta and bread from the wood-fired ovens in the town of Genzano are both for sale at Antica Caciara Trasteverina in Via San Francesco a Ripa, along with the best wines and *salumi.* You'll also find every kind of sandwich, pizza, and *dolce.* This is also the area to come to meet friends at a hip café.

Amid the exuberance you'll find some very good places for fine, but not fancy, dining. Ristorante Paris, in the small Piazza San Calisto, between Piazza San Cosimato and Piazza di Santa Maria in Trastevere, features both Jewish and traditional Roman *quinto quarto* dishes (page 143), as well as excellent fish. Checco er Carettiere offers traditional, stick-to-the-ribs Roman fare (don't miss the *supplì* and other fried dishes) near Ponte Sisto, the pedestrian bridge. Just above the heart of Trastevere, atop the Gianicolo (Janiculum Hill), opposite the Porta di San Pancrazio, is perhaps the area's most stylish restaurant, L'Antico Arco, known for serving superb cutting edge cuisine that mixes the traditional with the avant garde.

Centro Storico

The famous outdoor market in Piazza Campo de' Fiori is the gastronomic heart of one of the most archaeologically interesting areas of Rome's centre, covering several small *rioni*. Unlike the Forum area, where the archaeology is strictly delineated, the area extending from the Pantheon and Piazza Navona south to the Tiber and just east to the Theatre of Marcellus is itself one big archaeological site, with the ancient remains enclosed and embedded in the fabric of the medieval, Renaissance, and modern city.

Fortunately, you will find plenty to eat as you try – perhaps less successfully – to trace the outlines of the first century BC Theatre of Pompey in the curving streets that lie just east of the Campo de' Fiori, or as you contemplate the origins of the granite fountains of Piazza Farnese (the Baths of Caracalla).

In the photogenic, fountain-filled Piazza Navona, itself an ancient racetrack, posh café Tre Scalini serves the famous *tartufo* (ice cream truffle) that it invented. Visit the streets around the Pantheon, Rome's best preserved ancient temple, for excellent gelato (try Fiocco di Neve or the wonderful flavours at Giolitti) and the famous coffee at bars Sant'Eustachio and Tazza d'Oro (page 34). Trattoria Armando, with a menu that changes frequently and superb desserts, and the elegant seafood specialist Ristorante La Rosetta are two outstanding restaurants in the area.

Narrow, pedestrian-only Via dei Giubbonari is home to both the city's best fried salt cod, at the little Filettaro Santa Barbara, and charming Roscioli, a delica-tessen-cum-restaurant. From there it's a step across Via Arenula to the Jewish quarter (Rione XI) and the Antico Forno del Ghetto, a hole-in-the-wall kosher bakery known for the most formidable ricotta cake in town. You don't have to go to the Ghetto for fried artichokes, but lunch at Piperno, in Via Monte de' Cenci, or at nearby Da Giggetto, is a good excuse for a walk along the Via del Portico d'Ottavia, which has some of the capital's oldest continuously inhabited buildings.

Testaccio

Architecturally, Testaccio, Rione XX, which lies along the Tiber just south of the city centre, is relatively new. Most buildings in the area were built during or after an 1873 zoning plan that turned the former river port and open space into a workers' quarter of public housing and factories. The neighbourhood takes its name from the nickname of an archaeological site, a large hill of broken but neatly stacked amphorae dating from the fourth century.

It was, however, the *mattatoio*, or abbatoir, built between 1888 and 1891, that gave the quarter its modern association with food and eating, thanks to the trattorias that prepared appetizing recipes using *il quinto quarto,* the lesser cuts of meat and offal given to the workers as part of their pay. The abbatoir is still standing, with the allegorical sculpture group that includes a proud ox over its entrance (page 143), and has been put to various uses over the years.

The trattorias are still there, too, though most of them cater to a younger, more fashionable crowd than even ten or twenty years ago. Checchino dal 1887, in Via di Monte Testaccio, has been in business for more than a century, as its name attests, serving guests the finest Piedmontese cheeses after their tripe and *coda alla vaccinara* (oxtail stew). Da Oio a Casa Mia, in Via Galvani; Da Bucatino, in Via Luca della Robbia; and Agustarello, in Via Giovanni Branca, are among the Testaccio trattorias that offer economical versions of the neighbourhood classics. Those who want to eat something lighter can have a snack at Volpetti Più, a *tavola calda* offering eat-in versions of many of the prepared foods – such as pizza, *supplì, baccalà alla romana,* stuffed courgettes, and much more – sold at the well-stocked Volpetti shop in Via Marmorata.

Prati

Sometimes it seems as though the people who assigned the street names in Rome had a sense of humour. Thus one of the broad avenues that runs from the Tiber to near the Vatican is named Via Cola di Rienzo, after the fourteenth-century popular leader who tried to wrest temporal rule of Rome from the pope and nobles. This is Prati (literally "meadows"); its gracious grid plan dates to the years after 1870, when Rome had just become capital of the united Italy.

Locals come to the area, and especially Via Cola di Rienzo, for artisanal foods to take home or to provide sustenance while they make the rounds of the neighbourhood's famous shopping. Some Romans won't eat a spit-roasted chicken unless it comes from Franchi, the combination delicatessen and *tavola calda* at number 200. Others won't make a pot of coffee without their favourite blend from Castroni, next door at number 196. Prati's covered market is another popular draw thanks to the excellent fruit, vegetables, and other foods available, and also because of its distinctive white 1928 structure. The market is referred to as Piazza dell'Unità, but

the "piazza" is actually a stretch of the same Via Cola di Rienzo. Many Romans swear by the historic Gelateria Pellacchia, at number 103 in the same street, founded in 1904 and still whipping cream by hand.

Monti and Esquilino

The large swathe of the city extending roughly from the line between the Colosseum and the Basilica of San Giovanni in Laterano north to the Termini station corresponds approximately to two *rioni,* Monti and Esquilino. Wedged between Via Cavour and Via Nazionale are the narrow streets of Monti, which in antiquity was known as Suburra, and was a notorious slum. Further towards Termini are the broad avenues of the Esquilino. There, amid roomy four- and five-story *palazzi* built in the late nineteenth and early twentieth centuries, new immigrants from Asia and Africa are opening up many shops and restaurants.

Gastronomically, the whole area is dominated by the Piazza Vittorio market (page 22). The gourmet apex of the neighbourhood is Ristorante Agata e Romeo, on everyone's list of Rome's top restaurants. The small, down-to-earth Trattoria Monti, around the corner in Via San Vito, serves dishes from the Marche region, north-east of Rome. In Via Merulana, within sight of the Basilica of Santa Maria Maggiore, the breads and sweets of Panella draw customers from all over town, while down in Monti, Pizzeria Leonina (Via Leonina) serves exceptional pizza *al taglio* cut into neat squares on wooden boards. If there is one place that makes the whole neighbourhood smile, it's gelateria Fassi, located under the shaded porticoes of once-grand Piazza Vittorio Emanuele. This area is a bit run down now, and can be dangerous at night due to its proximity to Termini station. Nonetheless, it is worth making the trek out here for a visit to Fassi, more of an ice-cream parlour than a *gelateria,* and much beloved by locals and visitors alike since 1928.

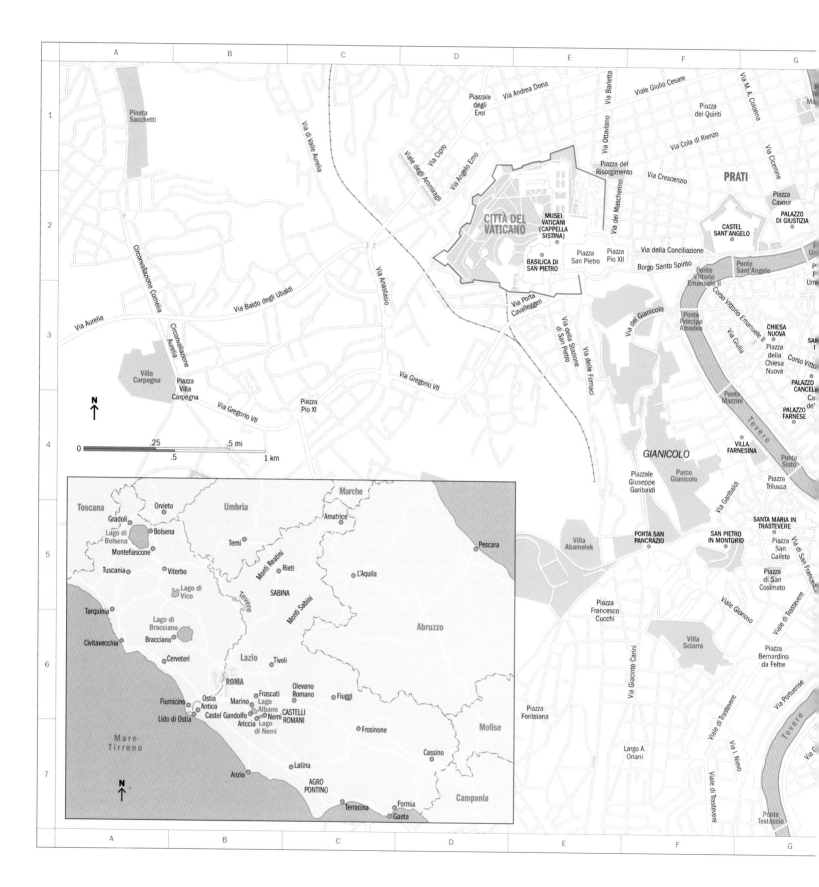

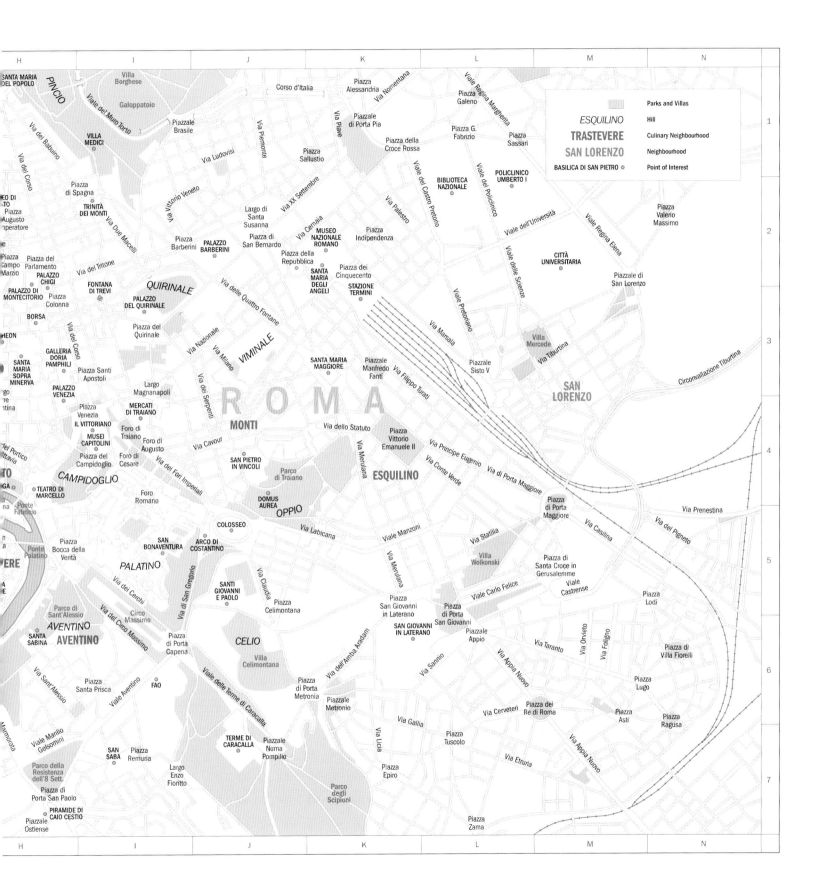

Best of **ROME**

Whether it is served *lungo, ristretto, tiepido, bollente, macchiato, zuccherato,* or *amaro*, coffee in Rome is some of the best in the world. What makes it taste so good? It's not the air, the water, the machines, or even the roast. It's the human factor – the magic touch of an expert *barista.*

COFFEE

Coffee drinking, or at least proximity to it, is inseparable from life in Rome. It's probably not an exaggeration to say that most relationships in Rome begin with an invitation for coffee. Working people may pay several visits to a coffee bar each day, and everyone does well to become known at a local bar, which can serve as a place to leave a letter, pick up a key, or hear the latest neighbourhood news.

When it comes to buying ground beans for home use, Romans are not so much coffee experts (though many are) as coffee partisans. There may be a perfectly good bar right next door, but they'll take a bus across town to buy a few days' worth at a favourite coffee roaster (invariably also a bar), because nothing else will do. On the return trip, the passengers on the bus will know that another coffee lover is on his or her way home with a bag of fine

powder that was freshly ground from beans roasted nearly black. The importance of a perfect cup of coffee at home is evidenced by the array of sizes of top-of-the-hob coffeemakers. Two cups are never made in a four-cup coffeepot, and many people even have a one-cup pot for perfect solo servings.

Don't ask for a latte at a Roman bar unless you want a glass of milk. Coffee with hot milk, usually served at home in an extra large cup or, at bars, in a glass, is *caffelatte.* When it is in a cup, with milk steamed to produce a head of froth, it is a cappuccino, or *cappuccio* in local vernacular. Both are really considered breakfast drinks, though a cappuccino is acceptable throughout the day. However, only tourists ask for a cappuccino after a meal. (Italians believe that too much milk after a meal is bad for the digestion.) If

you can't do without a touch of milk in your espresso, ask for a *caffè macchiato* (literally, "spotted"). For the same with cold milk, ask for a *caffè macchiato freddo.*

The customers at Italian bars will specify the desired temperature (*bollente,* "boiling", or *tiepido,* "lukewarm"), container (*tazza,* "cup", or *al vetro,* "in glass"), and degree of froth (*poca schiuma,* "not much foam") when they order. They also specify volume: *ristretto* is a more concentrated espresso; a *caffè lungo* is made with extra water; a *doppio* is a double espresso. None of these comes anywhere near the large volume or thin consistency of a *caffè americano,* which should be ordered only in international hotels, if at all.

Espresso spiked with a drop of brandy, grappa, or Sambuca (the Roman anise-flavoured liqueur) is called a *caffè corretto,*

In Rome, a frothy caffelatte is considered a breakfast drink.

which means "corrected". Post-prandial coffees are always served after, not with, dessert. A digestif served after (not with) the coffee is called *ammazzacaffè* ("coffee killer").

The word bar in Rome means, first, a coffee bar. But not everyone is addicted to caffeine, or even likes coffee. A *caffè d'orzo* (barley) is a coffee-like brew with the consistency of thin home-made coffee. More often customers will ask for a *decaffeinato* (five syllables) or a Hag (pronounced "ahg"), a popular brand. Bars also serve a range of medicinal-flavoured aperitifs and digestifs,

For the complete Roman bar experience, stand at the counter, elbow to elbow with the other patrons. Most bars have two price lists, one for counter service and one for table service. But if you would prefer to sit, don't be put off by the markup for a table. After all, a cup of coffee is a small price to pay when you need a place to rest or meet someone without being hurried away.

Coffee connoisseurs should be sure to visit bars that roast their own beans (look for the word *torrefazione,* which roughly means "roastery"). Unless advertised as 100 per

If there is one institution that encapsulates the quality of life in Rome, it is the bustling neighbourhood coffee bar.

along with the everyday spirits, for which, however, there is less demand. They also offer hot chocolate (mainly a morning drink) and a variety of teas – both caffeinated and decaffeinated.

The secondary business of a bar is to serve assorted other drinks, some alcoholic and some not, and snack foods of vastly varying degrees of interest, from often limp pastries to the most fascinating arrays of sandwiches and sweets. Occasionally a neighbourhood bar will also offer hot food, served buffet or even restaurant style. These simple meals can make for a satisfying and inexpensive quick lunch.

Visitors should make an effort to rise early and have a cappuccino and *cornetto* (the local croissant) with the crowds going to work. Both will taste better and cost much less than a hotel breakfast. But more important, the buzz of activity in the bar hits its peak in the morning, so it's a good idea to stop in early and fuel up, especially if you plan to spend the rest of the day walking around the city and standing in museums and churches, which can be quite exhausting.

cent arabica, the coffee itself is probably a *miscela* (blend) of arabica and robusta beans, as many people like the extra caffeine kick of robusta. Popular national coffee brands that appear frequently in Roman bars include Lavazza, from Turin; Kimbo, from Naples; and Illy Caffè, which is from Trieste.

Every Rome guidebook mentions the tiny, always crowded Caffè Sant'Eustachio, with its extra-creamy espresso, and the historic Tazza d'Oro, both near the Pantheon. Caffè Sant'Eustachio serves its coffee already sweetened with plenty of sugar. If you prefer no sugar, you have to say so when ordering. Both bars make outstanding coffee granitas topped with *panna montata* (whipped cream).

Many bars are just as busy, but not quite as famous. Cafffè Camerino (with three f's), in Largo Argentina, is practically an archetype. Loyal clientele from the neighbourhood flock there for coffee beans (freshly ground or whole), sweets of all kinds to take home, superb sandwiches, and a profusion of chocolate Easter eggs or whatever is in season. Most important, the *baristi* know how to make excellent coffee.

Alberto Sordi, playing a would-be American in the film *Un Americano a Roma* (1954), eyes his mother's spaghetti and growls, "Maccherone, m'hai provocato . . . e io me te magno." (Pasta, you are so provocative . . . and I'm going eat you up.) The hero then abandons himself to pleasure.

PASTA

Alberto Sordi was the quintessential Roman actor, and his great genius was his ability to embody the postwar everyman. In the much-loved scene quoted above, the Romans laugh with him, not at him. Now, as then, pasta is what you eat at mamma's kitchen table and also what you order at a fancy restaurant. It's what makes a meal a meal. All pretense collapses before it.

Countless other foods are at its service. Vegetables – courgettes, artichokes, various broccolis – have a double life as pasta sauces when sautéed with garlic and a little chilli. The sauce from *coda alla vaccinara* (page 143) may be even more delicious the next day served over *tonnarelli* (fresh square-cut spaghetti). Ricotta and spinach achieve harmony as the stuffing for ravioli. Beans and chick-peas are often mixed with pasta to make some of Rome's favourite dishes, such as *pasta e ceci* (page 93).

Pasta varies in composition, shape, and manufacture. It can be fresh or dried, made with or without eggs. The dough may be rolled and cut (by hand or machine) or extruded through dies. The flour can be *grano tenero* (soft wheat), *grano duro* or *semola* (hard wheat), or other grains: *grano saraceno* (buckwheat), *farro* (emmer), *riso* (rice), and *mais* (maize). Shapes can be long or short, and different types call for different sauces.

When making fettuccine and other pasta at home, it helps to have a hand-cranked machine that rolls and cuts the dough into neat strips. Some traditional home-made pastas, however, are made by hand. These include odd shapes such as *strozzapreti* (priest stranglers) and *stracci* (rags).

Most Roman neighbourhoods have a little shop that sells freshly made fettuccine, *tonnarelli*, tortellini, ravioli, and – especially on Thursdays – gnocchi. Many of these shops also offer a small selection of packaged dried pastas and sauce ingredients. Some pasta makers draw their customers from all over Rome with their original creations. Grand Gourmet, in the Flaminio quarter north of the centre, is known for jumbo *tortelli,* stuffed with, among other things, cheese and pears or *speck* (smoke-cured pork) and radicchio. Cellini, in the modern EUR quarter, sells specialities of other regions, such as *vincisgrassi* (a sort of lasagne), typical of the Marche, and *stringozzi* (long thick pasta) from Umbria. Franciosi, in the Appio quarter just outside the walls, is known for gnocchi flavoured with *ortiche* (nettles).

For Romans, a meal without pasta is like a day without sunshine.

The world of pasta does not split neatly into industrial and home-made. Many shops selling fresh pasta rely on a method that falls somewhere between the two. Large machines are typically used to mix, extrude, and roll the dough, but it is often shaped and finished by hand.

Choosing pasta

The starting point for choosing a good dried pasta is the label. The best pasta is made in Italy of only semolina flour and water and has been extruded through *trafile di bronzo* (bronze dies), which gives it a rough surface that helps it absorb the sauce. If dried pasta is bright yellow, it has probably been extruded through plastic or Teflon dies. Many artisanal or small manufacturers, such as Latini and Benedetto Cavalieri, dry their pasta slowly at low temperatures, which adds to the quality.

Who invented pasta?

Grain was first cultivated some nine thousand years ago. It was only a matter of time before someone thought to grind it into flour, mix it with water, shape it, and dry it.

Al-Idrisi, the Arab court geographer to Roger II of Sicily, reported in 1138 that the residents of Trabia, near Palermo, dried and exported strands of dough they called *itriya*, Arabic for "string". Records from Genoa dated 1244 and from the Anjou court in Naples dated 1295 show similar activity.

By the mid-fourteenth century, the Bolognese tradition of fresh pasta was under way. Then, in the 1830s, the modern age of dried commercial pasta began in Naples, along with the practice of cooking it al dente and serving it with a tomato sauce. Experimentation with shapes began early. Dozens of antique pasta machines, as well as the shapes they made, are on display at the small pasta museum, the Museo Nazionale delle Paste Alimentari, near the Quirinal Palace.

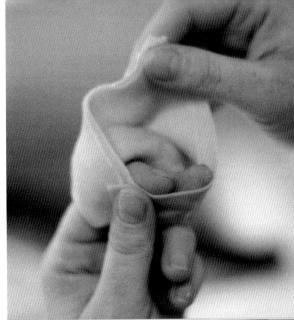

Making tortelloni

MIXING Equal amounts of soft-wheat and hard-wheat flours, a little salt, and eggs are mixed together by machine and then kneaded for about 10 minutes. Water is added – just enough for the dough to form walnut-sized balls.

ROLLING The dough is shifted to a second compartment in the machine, from which it is extruded and spooled on to rollers. Sheets are cut from the spooled dough. They are passed through a second machine for rolling, emerging about three times longer and nearly paper thin. Pieces

of speck (smoke-cured pork) are put through a mincer and mixed with mascarpone and Parmesan to make the filling.

FILLING AND SHAPING A pasta sheet is trimmed to a neat rectangle, brushed with egg yolk, and scored into squares. A dollop of filling is placed on each square, the squares are cut apart, each square is folded into a triangle, and the edges are pressed to seal. Finally, the two far points of the triangle are brought together, while the third point is curled outwards like the peak of a soft cap.

TORTELLONI

BUCATINI

CAPPELLETTI

MALTAGLIATI

TORTELLONI

In Rome ravioli are usually square and filled with a spinach and ricotta mixture, while *agnolotti,* usually semi-circular, are filled with meat. Handmade stuffed pastas in less conventional shapes and extra large sizes are called *tortelli* or *tortelloni.* A fluffy ricotta filling is perfect with the extra tender pasta of *tortelloni,* though the form also lends itself to creative fillings, such as pear and cheese or radicchio and *speck.* Like ravioli, *tortelloni* can be served with a simple tomato sauce or with melted butter, sage leaves, and freshly grated Parmesan.

BUCATINI

Bucatini are thick spaghetti pierced down the middle by a narrow hole. What good is such a small hole? The risk with any thick shape is that the outside could cook to a mush while the inside remains crunchy. The hole allows the water to penetrate to the core so the pasta will cook evenly. In Rome *bucatini* are almost always served *all'amatriciana* or *alla gricia.* They are difficult to eat with dignity: meant to be twirled like spaghetti, the strands fight back by hurling flecks of tomato sauce at the diner's shirt.

CAPPELLETTI

Christmas isn't Christmas without a full-bodied capon broth and plenty of small, meat-filled *cappelletti.* The name means "little hats", with specific reference to a type of floppy medieval hat. The shape is usually associated with the tortellini of the Emilia-Romagna region, where it originated. Technically the dough for *cappelletti* is a bit more robust and the exact composition of the meat filling varies. *Cappelletti* used to be eaten frequently with rich cream sauces, but today they are usually found only in broth.

MALTAGLIATI

The neat rhomboids into which commercially made *maltagliati* are cut belie their name, which means "badly cut". There are two kinds of *maltagliati:* those cut neatly but on the bias, either manufactured or home-made, and those truer to their name, the scraps of any kind of pasta dough left over after ravioli, fettuccine, and lasagne have been cut into their uniform shapes. Both types can be cooked and sauced as for any short pasta shape, but in Rome they are often mixed with chick-peas or beans in hearty soups such as *pasta e ceci* (page 93).

ORECCHIETTE

PENNE

RIGATONI

SPAGHETTI

ORECCHIETTE

Although this shape, called "little ears", is associated with the south of Italy, it is quite popular in Rome. The dough is made from either all hard wheat flour, or half hard and half soft wheat, and water. Neither extruded nor rolled and cut, they represent a third technique of pasta making: rolling and poking. Small handfuls are pulled from a ball of dough and rolled into cylinders, which are cut into small pieces. Each piece is poked with a thumb and drawn against the work surface until concave. *Broccoletti* (page 45) are their natural partner.

PENNE

Penna means "quill" and it is easy to see where bias-cut penne get their name. The short pasta can be found both smooth surfaced (*liscie*) and ridged (*rigate*). This versatile shape almost certainly migrated north from Campania, but penne are probably Rome's most popular all-purpose dried short pasta, often tossed with vegetable-based sauces such as *broccolo romanesco* (page 44), asparagus, or artichokes. They are obligatory in the dish *penne all'arrabbiata*, a simple but delicious Roman speciality of tomatoes, garlic, chilli, and parsley.

RIGATONI

A major player in the world of short formats, rigatoni are characterised by a large hole, 1 cm (½ inch) or more in diameter. Relatively thick and sturdy, they take about twice as long to cook as spaghetti. They get their name from the striations – *riga* means "straight line" – that cover the outer surface. Rigatoni are well suited to sauces that combine solids and liquid. In Rome the typical accompaniment is a tomato sauce with *la pagliata,* the intestines of a milk-fed calf. *Mezzemaniche* and *bombolotti* are similar, but shorter, shapes popular in Rome.

SPAGHETTI

When you tie up a packet you use *spago* (twine), and indeed spaghetti are nothing more than strings of hard wheat flour and water. The king of pasta shapes, spaghetti can range in diameter from 1.7 to 2 mm (less than $\frac{1}{16}$ inch). Any smaller and a second diminutive suffix turns it into *spaghettini*. Spaghetti is at its best with oil-based or relatively thin sauces that easily coat the long strands, such as *alle vongole* (with clams) or *pomodoro e basilico* (with tomato and basil).

Wild borage, deep green chard, crisp lettuces, pink-tinged spinach, crunchy *puntarelle*, and an abundance of broccolis and chicories – the array of greens (and reds, yellows, and oranges) makes the Roman vegetable markets among the most exciting sights in a city hardly lacking in visual interest.

GREENS

Most Romans like broccoli – and *broccoletti* – and spinach, chard, cauliflower, and Brussels sprouts. It is easy to get people to eat their vegetables because greens just taste better in Rome. They are sweeter and milder, yet more flavourful at the same time. That is true whether the greens are home-grown or brought in from warmer regions, including Sicily, Sardinia, Apulia, and Campania.

Still, vegetables grown near Rome, which bear the label *romanesco,* are considered the most desirable. Until well into the 1980s, one of the most striking features as you drove out of Rome was the abrupt switch from urban centre to rural area. That rapidly shrinking countryside, the immediate outskirts of Rome, especially extending to the south-east into the Alban Hills, is the *campagna romana,* immortalised in generations of Grand Tour paintings typically populated by peasants in colourful clothes with aprons, brimmed hats, and baskets. Their spiritual, and in some cases actual, descendants – unfortunately fewer and fewer of them – still gather wild chicories, cresses, lettuces, borage, and herbs to sell in town at the large and small municipal markets that serve every neighbourhood. Urban sprawl, however, is taking its toll.

Rome's splendid climate, which can hover above freezing for at most a few weeks each winter, but rarely goes below it, produces magnificent leafy greens, both domesticated and wild, all winter. Wild salad greens, sold collectively as *misticanza* or *insalata di campo* (field greens), are hand gathered by sharp-eyed, experienced pickers. While globalisation and greenhouses make soft fruits like straw-berries and tomatoes available year round, the fresh produce at the city markets punctuates the seasons better than any calendar. When the big, round artichokes from Cerveteri, just north of Rome, take over from the smaller Sardinians in March, it's time to think about making *carciofi alla giudia* (page 52). In a few weeks the dish on every cook's menu will be *la vignarola* (page 94), because broad beans and peas will start coming along. Asparagus is available year round nowadays, but its peak season is still spring. The beautiful fluted *zucchine romanesche* are in the markets by late winter, but smart shoppers wait to buy, because when the weather turns torrid, *zucchine* (courgettes), peppers, and auber-gines are plentiful and become the pillars of the local cuisine. In summer, Rome is filled with tomatoes too, which are cooked into sauces or eaten raw in salads.

A wealth of greens and other vegetables nourishes Romans year round.

BROCCOLO ROMANESCO

CICORIA SELVATICA

MISTICANZA ROMANA

LATTUGA ROMANA

BROCCOLO ROMANESCO

The Roman variety of what in Italian is properly called *cavolo broccolo romanesco* is found principally in the winter. It looks like a chartreuse cauliflower with strange pointed florets, but the taste is nearer broccoli. The florets are delicious simply boiled or steamed and dressed with olive oil and a squeeze of lemon, or deep-fried as part of a *fritto misto*. They can also be boiled and sautéed, like *cicoria* and *broccoletti,* or served on pasta. The most emblematic use of *broccolo* in Roman cooking is in *minestra di arzilla con pasta e broccoli* – skate broth with *broccolo* and spaghetti.

CICORIA SELVATICA

Gathered in the countryside in the cooler months, wild chicory grows in exuberant heads with lots of almost curly, saw-toothed leaves. The flavour ranges from pleasantly bitter to very bitter indeed. The leaves should be rinsed and trimmed like spinach and then dropped into a large pan of boiling salted water and cooked until quite tender. In Rome those with strong palates will eat boiled wild chicory cold with olive oil and lemon juice, but most people prefer to sauté the boiled greens with garlic and chilli.

MISTICANZA ROMANA

The term *misticanza* is regularly applied to various assortments of greens, from mild combinations that recall Provençal mesclun to banal bags of ready-made salads to robust blends of spiky, hairy wild things that must be boiled to be edible. To connoisseurs, however, *la misticanza romana* is a wild salad of considerable character and exquisite charm. The mix, gathered in the countryside in wintertime, will vary, but may include wild chicory, salad burnet, wood sorrel, borage, endive, and poppy greens. It is usually dressed with only vinegar and olive oil.

LATTUGA ROMANA

Caesar salad is creeping on to Italian menus – and no wonder, with such tender and flavourful cos lettuces available. In Rome cos is called simply *lattuga* (lettuce). In the vernacular of the Roman vegetable market, the generic term for salad greens is *insalata* rather than *lattuga,* which is reserved for cos lettuce only. It is used as any salad green, but unlike other lettuces, it can also be cooked, as an addition to *la vignarola* (page 94), or braised on its own and served as a *contorno*.

BROCCOLETTI

RUGHETTA SELVATICA

SPINACI

PUNTARELLE

BROCCOLETTI

Broccoletti, which are available principally in the cooler months, are like broccoli whose leaves have grown and whose florets have shrunk. Roman greengrocers carefully trim off the tough ends, then peel and split the remaining stalks. *Broccoletti* are used in much the same way as the similar *cime di rapa* or *brocco-letti di rapa* (turnip tops): both make an excellent addition to pasta, or they can be served as a side dish, briefly boiled and dressed with olive oil and lemon juice.

RUGHETTA SELVATICA

In Italian it is *ruchetta,* in Rome it is *rughetta selvatica.* Although best translated as wild rocket, a truly analogous plant may not exist out-side Italy. Available all year, *rughetta* has a bitter, peppery flavour. Despite the name, most of the *rughetta selvatica* sold is cultivated, but sharp eyes will find it growing even in the city. It's often mixed with cherry tomatoes or with other greens for a salad, but is delicious on its own too, or combined with sliced spring onions and shaved Parmesan.

SPINACI

People who think they don't like spinach should not give up until they have tasted it in Italy. Mainly available in winter, it reaches the market young and tender, enticingly pink at the base of the stalks, the smallest leaves almost emerald. The whole leaves are usually steamed and then served with butter or with lemon and olive oil. It can also be sautéed with raisins and pine nuts. Spinach is an essential ingredient in classic ravioli when mixed with ricotta. The smallest leaves are often separated out and sold for salads.

PUNTARELLE

The fresh, slightly bitter taste of this *romanissima* salad green is reason enough to visit the Eternal City in winter. With the first warm weather, the stalks of *puntarelle,* a type of Catalonian chicory, grow woody, and won't be seen again until the first chill of autumn. In Rome *puntarelle* are always served with a dressing made with anchovy and garlic (page 160). Preparation begins with the special cut. The outer leaves and tough bases of the hollow stalks are removed, then each stalk is carefully peeled and split lengthways into several strips.

A crisp focaccia with prosciutto, a flat bread 2 metres (6 feet) long, a rectangle of dough strewn with sliced potatoes, a canapé, a pie, and a crisp round base topped with sliced tomatoes and mozzarella: in Rome, they all come under the term *pizza*.

PIZZA

In the relatively rigid programme that represents the Italian gastronomic day or week, pizza is usually the main item of a light meal served in a dedicated pizzeria. It is usually washed down with beer, light white wine, or a soft drink and may be preceded by bruschetta (page 69), *supplì* (page 73), deep-fried salt cod fillets, or another snack, usually fried. When the pizzeria also serves other dishes, the pizza may be treated as a *primo piatto,* that is, a substitute for pasta or soup.

On Sunday evenings, Rome's pizzerias are filled with families. The rest of the week, the customers tend to be young people who want to *stare insieme* (pass the time together), or groups of adults who want an evening out that is not *impegnativo* (a big commitment).

The best pizzas come from wood-burning ovens, which are rarely fired up before dark in Rome's warm climate, making it easier to find a pizza for dinner than for lunch. The Roman pizza base is thin and fairly crisp, though tender enough to be eaten – as is proper – with knife and fork. The border is narrow and low. As with pasta, the base should not be viewed as merely a vehicle for the topping. A naked pizza – the Roman focaccia – drizzled with olive oil and perhaps adorned with some diced tomatoes or a slice or two of prosciutto, is proof of that.

The yeasty Neapolitan base, with its wide, high border, has been making inroads in Rome, but this is probably the only identifiably external influence. Pizza toppings include old classics, new classics, and idiosyncrasies of individual pizzerias. Pies topped with *mozzarella di bufala* and Pachino tomatoes (prized cherry tomatoes from south-eastern Sicily), *fiori di zucca* (courgette flowers), or *rughetta* (rocket) have all joined *pizza alla napoletana* (anchovies, tomatoes, and mozzarella), *pizza ai funghi* (fresh mushrooms, tomatoes, and mozzarella), and *pizza Margherita* (tomatoes, mozzarella, and sometimes basil) as near-universal menu items.

One of the best places in Rome to find thin, crusty pizza is Da Baffetto, near Piazza Navona. At Pizzeria Ivo in Trastevere, pizzas come in two sizes (large and larger), and a trattoria menu is also available. Both Da Baffetto and Ivo have plenty of atmosphere, but for the quintessential Roman pizzeria experience – lots of bustle, no-frills decor, outdoor seating in summer, and the best thin, crispy base – you can't beat Ai Marmi, also in Trastevere, known popularly as "*l'obitorio*" (the morgue) because of its marble tables.

Naples invented it, but Rome has perfected thin, crusty pizza.

High on the list of things that make Romans proud is *pizza bianca* – literally, "white pizza" – the sublime flat bread that is white and soft inside and golden brown and crisp on top. When the pizza is filled with ripe figs and prosciutto, a local favourite, it is called *pizza e fichi,* a term that has come to mean "as good as it gets" in local parlance.

Popular fillings

Pizza bianca is often eaten plain, preferably just out of the oven, but almost every café in town offers it split horizontally and filled as a sandwich. Most Romans like it stuffed with ripe fresh figs and prosciutto. But the fig season is short. *Mortadella* or prosciutto and fresh mozzarella is a classic, while *bresaola* (air-dried beef) and *rughetta* (rocket), with or without shaved Parmesan, is decidedly modern. Tuna and marinated artichoke hearts is also a time tested and delicious combination.

Where to find pizza bianca

Just about every *panificio* (bakery) in town bakes *pizza bianca* and every local café sells it and will fill it with something easy. Shops that serve *pizza al taglio* (by the slice) often also sell *pizza bianca* filled with sautéed greens or other ingredients. Two good ones to try are Pizzeria Leonina, in the street of the same name near Via Cavour, and Pizzeria Florida, in Largo Argentina. But true aficionados go to the cafés that specialise in *pizza bianca* cut and filled to order.

At Frontoni, in Viale Trastevere, no one will bat an eyelid at unusual requests. *Puntarelle* paired with salami? Certainly. Aubergine and smoked mozzarella? No problem. Roscioli, in Via dei Chiavari, fills its superb pizza with simpler fare, such as *bresaola* (air-dried beef). The ultimate is the famed Antico Forno in Piazza Campo de' Fiori, which opened a separate shop to sell its ready-stuffed *pizza bianca* with fillings such as courgette flowers and mozzarella.

Making pizza bianca

MIXING For each batch of *pizza bianca*, flour, water, salt, and fresh yeast are put into a giant mixer, which first combines the ingredients and then kneads them to yield a smooth, elastic dough. The dough is left to rise in a warm place for up to 6 hours.

SHAPING AND KNEADING The risen dough is cut into portions, each weighing about 2 kg (4 lb). Each piece is shaped by hand into a 60-cm (24-inch) loaf, then sprinkled with flour and left to rest for about 15 minutes. The loaves are then

kneaded and stretched. After being worked for about 5 minutes, the dough emerges as a slim shape approximately 2 metres (6 feet) long. The pizza's characteristic dimpled surface is made by the baker's fingertips, which work over the surface as if they were playing a piano.

BAKING The pizzas are brushed with olive oil and transferred on a long, narrow *pala* (peel) to the oven, where they bake at 260°C (500°F) for about 10 minutes or until crisp and golden. They are then slipped on to a shelf and left to cool.

Artichokes seasoned and plunged into hot oil, courgette flowers filled with mozzarella, deep-fried salt cod fillets, and ricotta desserts are all associated with the traditional table of Rome's Jewish community. Today, these dishes are almost inseparable from the popular cooking of the city.

CUCINA EBRAICA

A Jewish community has existed in Rome since at least the second century BC. The population numbered perhaps forty thousand at the height of the Roman Empire. Many Jews were brought to Rome as slaves captured in wars in Judaea in the first century AD. They lived in various parts of the city, especially in Trastevere. In the thirteenth century, the city's Jews were segregated in a few streets opposite the Tiber Island. Then, in 1555, a papal edict forced them to live within a ghetto with gates kept locked at night. It also mandated the closure of all but one synagogue, curtailed their civil rights, and severely limited their means of making a living. The gates remained until 1848.

La cucina ebraica, or "Jewish cooking", in the Roman context refers to the recipes developed by the small group of city dwellers who lived in this tiny, densely populated neighbourhood. Within the limits of their dietary laws and their poverty (shared with much of Rome), Jewish cooks are generally credited with having invented the city's *cucina povera* (peasant cooking). Deep-frying, still today the downfall of many Romans, gave flavour to ingredients that the wealthy spurned, like courgette flowers. Traditional recipes now seldom found outside the home include *indivia rehaminà* (chicory soup), *scaloppine con la lattuga* (veal with cos lettuce), and stuffed turkey neck. Other dishes, such as red mullet with raisins and pine nuts, considered a delicacy, and fresh anchovies baked with endive, do sometimes appear on restaurant menus.

Today, the Jewish quarter – it is still there, and now a property hot spot – is home to a plethora of good food shops and restaurants, though not all of them are kosher or even Jewish. Gentile Rome goes to the Ghetto, too, for outstanding kosher *pizza al taglio* (by the slice) and *panini* at Zi' Fenizia and for superb *torta di ricotta* (page 170) and *tozzetti* (page 173) at the Forno del Ghetto, the tiny bakery in Via del Portico d'Ottavia.

The most popular dishes from the *cucina ebraica* today are the *fritti:* deep-fried artichokes, courgette flowers, salt cod fillets, and bites of mozzarella and vegetables. In the quarter, elegant Piperno and venerable Da Giggetto, located right next to the ancient ruins of the Portico d'Ottavia, both serve excellent Jewish-Roman cuisine. Across the Tiber, in Trastevere, Ristorante Paris (a surname, not an allusion to France) produces an irresistible Jewish-style *fritto misto.*

The tiny Forno del Ghetto is famous for its cinnamon tozzetti.

Perhaps the most famous dish of the Roman Jewish repertoire is *carciofo alla giudia,* a deep-fried artichoke that is pressed flat until it resembles a flower dipped in bronze. The petals are crisp, which makes the tender heart almost a surprise. There's no batter or flour. The magic is in the expert preparation of the artichoke so that every bit is edible.

Artichoke varieties

Carciofo alla giudia achieves its greatest glory in late winter and early spring with the arrival of the Romanesco artichoke, a globe variety harvested around Rome. It is even better if it's also a *cimarolo,* from the *cima* (top) of the plant's main stalk. *Cimaroli* are larger than the artichokes from the side branches, and the top is slightly flattened. During most of winter, Rome's markets offer delicious, albeit smaller, specimens from warmer regions.

Fritti

Rome has a mass addiction to deep-frying. Morsels of food, some in *pastella* (batter), some in breadcrumbs, and some thrown naked into the hot oil, are served in various combinations at every level of the restaurant hierarchy. Bars, *rosticcerie, friggitorie* (fry shops), and pizzerias serve *supplì* (page 73) and *arancini* (rice balls).

A typical *fritti* combination will feature, in addition to artichokes, battered courgette flowers filled with mozzarella and anchovies,

nutmeg-scented potato croquettes, and crisp courgette spears. It is usually a good idea to skip the fried snacks at pizzerias and order them instead at *friggitorie* or fine restaurants. The *supplì* offered at the cafeteria-style Volpetti Più, in Testaccio, are excellent, as are the *fritti* at Checco er Carettiere, in Trastevere. But good *fritti* are not confined to the fancy establishments: the best *baccalà* (salt cod) fillets are at Filettaro Santa Barbara, which serves almost nothing else.

Making carciofi alla giudia

TRIMMING One of the most enviable skills of the Roman cook or greengrocer is the ability to trim a raw artichoke into a neat ball atop a smooth stalk, all edible. The outer leaves are pulled off, and the stalk is peeled. The artichoke is then rolled against a blade to remove the tips of the outer layer. Finally, the centre leaves and choke are dug out, and the artichokes are placed in water.

FRYING The damp artichokes are tossed vigorously with salt and pepper and dropped into a deep pot

of hot (170–180°C/330–350°F) olive oil to fry for about 20 minutes, then drained head down. Just before serving, the fried artichokes are dropped into fresh hot oil for a brief second frying.

PRESSING After the second frying, each artichoke is pressed gently, head down, between perforated metal discs to drain off the last drops of oil. This gives the artichoke its characteristic flower-like shape. From there, it goes directly to the plate, alone or as part of a *fritto misto*.

Gone are the days when the local carafe wine curled your hair and most bottles came from Tuscany. It is getting easier and easier to find good wine in Rome. Today, chic wine shops and wine bars with encyclopaedic lists have largely replaced the local barrel-and-carafe *osteria*.

WINE

The wines produced in Lazio, the region around Rome, are 80 per cent white, and almost all of the whites contain the native Trebbiano and Malvasia grapes. Led by Frascati, the most famous local appellation, Lazio's white wines have always been known for being low cost and easy to drink. Until the 1990s, they were rarely noted for their quality, but thanks to the efforts of a few dedicated producers, local whites are now poured in some of Rome's finest restaurants. Reds from the region, relying largely on either Sangiovese or international grape varieties, have also won greater recognition in recent years.

In Rome it is popular for new, hip wine establishments to go by the English term *wine bar*, rather than the traditional *fiaschetteria, bottiglieria,* or *osteria*. In the past, Italian towns boasted neighbourhood places where

patrons came to drink wine and socialise. The wine was drawn by spigot from barrels into glass carafes, and the available food was often just enough to keep the drinker upright – say, a hard-boiled egg. These places have evolved into slick operations serving interesting wines from every region in Italy, and even abroad, plus light meals and snacks.

Two excellent wine bars that led the way are Cavour 313, in Via Cavour near the Roman Forum, and Cul de Sac, in Piazza Pasquino, near Piazza Navona. The 'Gusto complex, in Piazza Augusto Imperatore, combines a pizzeria, kitchenware shop, and restaurant with a state-of-the-art wine bar. The first of the modern wine bars, Trimani, in Via Cernaia, near Termini station, is an adjunct to the adjacent wine shop of the same name. Anacleto Bleve's new wine bar, Casa

Bleve, near Piazza Navona, started almost by accident when he began serving a casual lunch at his older shop, located in the Ghetto.

There are three official quality designations for Italian wine. *Denominazione d'origine controllata* (DOC) is the basic designation, corresponding to the *appellation contrôlée* in France. It guarantees that the wine was both produced within a designated area and in keeping with specific criteria of composition and production. *Denominazione d'origine controllata e Garantita* (DOCG) is similar, with stricter controls. In the past, producers who found the DOC designation too restrictive had to label their bottles *vino da tavola* (table wine). Since 1992, *indicazione geografica tipica* (IGT) has provided a category for diverse blends and techniques tied to a specific area, but with less rigid specifications.

Both the red and white wines of Lazio have finally come into their own.

FRASCATI

MARINO DOC

EST! EST!! EST!!!
DI MONTEFIASCONE

CERVETERI

FRASCATI

Until the 1990s, straw-coloured Frascati DOC, a blend of native Malvasia and Trebbiano grapes, was considered an inexpensive, drinkable wine. Its fame depended on its sheer quantitative dominance of the region's production and on the beauty of the hill towns of the Castelli Romani, south-east of Rome, where the vineyards flourish. Many of its producers still go for quantity – now aided by modern techniques that make a drier, more uniform wine – but the single-vineyard Frascatis of some estates, such as Castel de Paolis and Villa Simone, are lovely, both floral and fruity.

MARINO DOC

Another DOC zone in the Castelli Romani, the Marino area produces wines that are similar in composition to adjacent Frascati. The zone is dominated by two names. One is the large, and largely mass-market, Gotta d'Oro. The other is the family business that put the Castelli on the modern oenological map, Colle Picchioni, founded in the 1970s by Paola Di Mauro. She and her son Armando still run the business. Bright gold Colle Picchioni Selezione Oro, a blend of Malvasia del Lazio, Trebbiano Giallo, Sémillon, and small amounts of other grapes, has notes of acacia flowers and apples.

EST! EST!! EST!!!
DI MONTEFIASCONE

This DOC white from the province of Viterbo is made of Trebbiano, Malvasia, and Rossetto grapes. It is best known for its amusing name, born of legend: in 1100, a German bishop travelling to Rome sent his servant ahead to find inns with wine fit to drink. He was to write "est" (Latin for "it is") on the door of acceptable inns. At Montefiascone, the servant found the wine to be so good that he wrote his recommendation in triplicate. Falesco's single-vineyard Poggio dei Gelsi, along with a few others, has brought dignity back to the denomination.

CERVETERI

Cerveteri is the name of a charming town north of Rome, near the Tyrrhenian Sea. It is a DOC zone and, perhaps most famously, an archaeological area containing historically important and beautiful Etruscan cemeteries. Wines have been produced in the area for hundreds of years, and the Etruscan method of training vines to trees, called *vite maritata,* is still found in parts of central Italy. The DOC designation covers both white and red, but the white (made from 50 per cent Trebbiano grapes, 35 per cent Malvasia, and smaller amounts of other varieties) is prevalent.

GRECHETTO   ROSSO LAZIO   CESANESE   ALEATICO DI GRADOLI

GRECHETTO

The Grechetto grape, one of central Italy's oldest varieties, is usually associated with Umbria but grows well in north-eastern Lazio. The award-winning Latour a Civitella, produced by Sergio Mottura and classified as Grechetto di Civitella d'Agliano IGT, is made entirely from Grechetto grapes grown near the town of Civitella d'Agliano, almost in Umbria. The bright gold wine is fermented in wood casks in ancient grottoes of volcanic tufa before spending ten more months in oak. More often Grechetto is mixed with Trebbiano, Verdello, and Malvasia, other native whites.

ROSSO LAZIO

The designation Rosso Lazio IGT is used for some of the region's finest and most innovative wines. The Di Mauro family's Vigna del Vassallo, a velvety Merlot blend, has earned "Three Glasses" (the maximum) in the prestigious *Gambero Rosso* classification. Other respected Lazio IGTs include Castel de Paolis's I Quattro Mori, made of Syrah, Merlot, Cabernet Sauvignon, and Petit Verdot; and Casale del Giglio's Mater Matuta, mostly Syrah with 15 per cent Petit Verdot. Falesco's Montiano is all Merlot, a favourite component of new Lazio reds.

CESANESE

Many of Lazio's best reds are made from French grape varieties, and others rely primarily on the native Montepulciano or Sangiovese. The local Cesanese grape, however, is used for dry and sweet wines in three DOC zones in the region's southernmost province, Frosinone. The wines, Piglio, Affile, and Olevano Romano, are a lovely ruby red when young. New uses are being found for this ancient grape. Concento IGT, a full-bodied Cesanese-Syrah blend made by L'Olivella, combines the more familiar taste of Syrah with an exotic hint of spiciness.

ALEATICO DI GRADOLI

Frascati and a few other local wines come in semisweet (*abboccato* or *amabile*) versions, but the region's only true dessert wine is the sweet, red Aleatico di Gradoli, from a small DOC zone in the province of Viterbo around the town of Gradoli. Made entirely from the black Aleatico grape, it is often likened to port in its *liquoroso* (fortified) version, accomplished through partially drying the grapes. Its destiny is to be served with hazelnut *tozzetti* (page 173), much as Vin Santo is paired with *cantucci* in Tuscany.

If you kept a close eye on a Roman's eating habits, from the first *cornetto* in the morning to the last *cioccolatino* in the evening, you might come away with a new understanding of the words "Mediterranean diet". Every religious holiday and season – indeed, nearly every hour of the day – has its own special *dolce*.

DOLCI

The *pasticceria* (pastry shop) may well be the most important retail establishment in Rome. It is practically the only place where you can buy a last-minute gift on Christmas morning or a gigantic chocolate egg at Easter. The word *dolce,* literally "sweet", covers both the dessert course of the meal and the item itself. The diminutive suffix is attached *(dolcetto)* when a sweet is small or when you are trying to pretend it isn't so sinful. The categories of Roman sweets range from the practically nutritious (biscotti made with milk, suitable for children's breakfasts) to the wicked by any standard, such as *maritozzi,* sweet buns cut in half and filled with whipped cream.

Ever since the earliest history of Rome, when patrician couples shared a spelt cake at their wedding, sweets have been closely associated with religious occasions, and

until the eighteenth century, they had to be ordered from convents or made at home. A list of typical Roman confections reads like a liturgical calendar: *colomba* (dove-shaped cake) for Easter, *frappe* (strips of fried dough) for carnival, *maritozzi quaresimali* (raisin buns) for Lent, *pangiallo* (fruit cake) for Christmas, *fave dolci* (almond biscuits) for All Souls' Day, and *bignè di San Giuseppe* (choux buns) for Saint Joseph's Day on 19th March, Italy's Father's Day.

Most neighbourhoods have a serviceable *pasticceria,* often connected with a bar. In the centre of Rome, the elegant *gelateria* Giolitti boasts a big pastry counter of profiteroles and other delicacies. Longer on charm than on polish, the venerable Valzani, in Trastevere, makes more traditional sweets, like *pangiallo* and the spicier *pampepato,* dense cakes

bursting with dried fruit and nuts; chewy *mostaccioli;* and *torrone* (nougat) encrusted with pine nuts. I Dolci di Checco er Carettiere, a spiffy new adjunct to an old restaurant near Ponte Sisto, also in Trastevere, makes everything from *cornetti* to éclairs and is also a fashionable place for coffee and snacks, despite its small size. Ciampini, in Piazza San Lorenzo in Lucina, in the heart of the Piazza di Spagna shopping district, provides tables indoors and out for patrons to indulge a sweet tooth, perhaps on miniature cones of gelato.

Every day is 14th February at the colourful and charming Moriondo e Gariglio, between Piazza Collegio Romano and the Pantheon, best known of a growing number of chocolate shops in Rome. (Summertime visitors should know, however, that many of these shops close completely for the season.)

Roman sweets vary from crunchy biscotti to fruit-filled tarts.

In the past, when families went on outings to the Castelli Romani, the hill towns south-east of Rome, they would bring their lunch from home. Once in the Castelli, however, they would buy bread and the various dry *dolci* that went well with a glass of the local sweet wine. The favourites among these sweets were the anise-flavoured rings called *ciambelline*.

Ciambelline and holidays

Ciambelline and the larger *ciambelle* have long figured in a handful of Catholic feast days. On the Feast of the Circumcision, 1st January, the Carmelite nuns of Velletri traditionally sent the town magistrate a basket of *ciambelle*. To honour Saint Blaise, patron of wool combers, *ciambelline* are still baked in every town in the province of Rome for his feast day, 3rd February. French-born Saint Roch is often depicted receiving his only food – a *ciambella* – from a dog.

Ancient Roman sweets

Ring-shaped sweets have been around at least since the Roman Empire. A recipe for a proto-doughnut in Apicius's *De re coquinaria*, the only surviving cookery book of the time, calls for moistening soft breadcrumbs with milk, forming the mixture into rings, frying them in oil, and then drizzling with honey.

Cane sugar was imported from Egypt but was far too costly for making sweets. Honey, from local bees or imported from the mountains of Greece, was the ancients' favourite sweetener.

A cooked-down grape must, called *defrutum,* was a popular, and cheaper, alternative.

Flaky pastry and fresh cheese were often combined, a partnership reminiscent of today's honey-drenched Greek and Near Eastern pastries. Largely alien to our modern palates, however, is the ancient custom of combining black pepper with sweet foods, such as fried dates rolled in pepper, and *tyropatina,* a rich custard made of milk, eggs, and honey and a dusting of pepper.

Making ciambelline al vino

BEATING THE DOUGH Sugar, olive oil, margarine or other fat, and red wine (though white wine is also an option) are *montati* (beaten) by machine to the consistency of whipped cream. Yeast and flour are added, and the dough is mixed and then kneaded for about 20 minutes.

ROLLING Knobs of dough are quickly rolled back and forth against the work surface into ropes about 20 cm (8 inches) long and 1.5 cm (²⁄₃ inch) in diameter. Any excess dough is pinched off and returned to the mass of unformed dough. In a

single, quick movement, the ends of each rope of dough are gently joined together (but not pressed), to form a ring.

DIPPING The resulting ring, which is about 9 cm (3½ inches) in diameter, is dipped on one side in granulated sugar and set, sugared side up, on a paper-lined baking tray.

BAKING The *ciambelline* are baked at 220°C (425°F) for 15–20 minutes or until golden. They are then removed from the oven and left to cool.

CASTAGNACCIO

CORNETTO

CANNOLI

MOSTACCIOLI

CIAMBELLINE AL VINO

CANNOLI

These Sicilian sweets par excellence have been enthusiastically adopted by Romans. They are made from wafers rolled to form large tubes (which *cannoli* roughly means), fried, and then filled with lightly sweetened ricotta. The wafer, called *scorza*, or "rind", contains cocoa and Marsala in addition to butter, eggs, and flour. The filling is almost pure ricotta with bits of candied pumpkin *(zuccata)*, chocolate, and sometimes pistachios (a product of Sicily). *Mignon*, or "bite-size", cannoli are favourites in the assortments (usually boxed up to take away) that Romans love so much.

CASTAGNACCIO

Castagna (chestnut) flour, sugar, olive oil, raisins, pine nuts, and rosemary go into this dense, flat cake, which resembles a pizza and is more of a snack than a dessert. Children used to buy *castagnaccio* from street vendors. Today, many *pizza al taglio* shops sell it by the slice, although it is also easy to make at home. It is popular in northern Lazio, Umbria, and Tuscany, an important zone for chestnut growing. The sweet is usually prepared in autumn and winter, when the nuts are harvested and milled, but it can be made any time of year if the flour has been properly stored to avoid it going rancid.

CORNETTO

Cappuccino and *cornetto* are the ritual way to start the Roman day, preferably in a busy bar. In the 1960s, Italian film director Nanni Loy raised the combination to the pantheon of iconic meals on the Italian version of the television show *Candid Camera,* when he dunked his *cornetto* in the cappuccino of strangers to film their astonishment. The shape of the Roman *cornetto* (*corno* means "horn") resembles a croissant, but is usually smaller. It can be filled with jam (usually apricot). A savoury version often comes filled with prosciutto.

MOSTACCIOLI

These chewy, diamond-shaped biscuits are now found in different versions throughout Italy, but they originated in Lazio. The name is believed to derive from the Latin *mustaceus,* a flat cake consumed at weddings in ancient Rome. *Mustum,* Latin for "grape must" (referring to the juice released before and during fermentation), provided sweetening as well as the name. The ingredients are flour, egg whites, honey, nuts, citrus peel, and candied and dried fruits. Some contemporary versions might include cocoa or chocolate.

CROSTATA DI FRUTTA

PANGIALLO

DIAVOLETTI AL PEPERONCINO

CROSTATA DI FRUTTA

SFOGLIATELLE

CIAMBELLINE AL VINO

Almost anything round can be called a *ciambella*, from a doughnut to a lifebelt, so the name tells us that these classic biscotti are going to be small and ring shaped. They are perfect at the end of a meal.

SFOGLIATELLE

Like Marilyn Monroe delighted to find new places to put diamonds, Romans just love new places to put ricotta. These delicacies, which are usually associated with Campania, are made by cutting and layering thin sheets of pastry, which are filled with a creamy combination of ricotta and semolina.

CROSTATA DI FRUTTA

Thick shortcrust pastry and a layer of preserved or fresh fruit are all it takes to assemble one of the most popular, and most flexible, of all Roman *dolci*. Sometimes the fruit tart is a quick solution for what to bring to a party; other times it is a showcase for home-made jams cooked from fruits harvested from the bounteous trees of a country house. Bars and pastry shops also offer individual tarts to have with tea, coffee, or perhaps a liqueur. Not traditionally a dessert, the *crostata* is properly eaten as a between-meal snack, often in the late afternoon.

PANGIALLO

The name *pangiallo,* literally "yellow bread", does not do justice to this delicious nut and fruit cake, traditionally baked in Lazio and Umbria at Christmastime. It is commonly made with a rich combination of hazelnuts, walnuts, almonds, pine nuts, raisins, dried figs, candied citron, orange peel, and spices. Like most sweets that can be picked up with the fingers, *pangiallo* is not so much a dessert as something to be enjoyed with coffee or sweet wine. Richer versions used to contain saffron-tinged almond paste, hence the name.

DIAVOLETTI AL PEPERONCINO

Not all Roman sweets have their origin in the mists of time. When the film *Chocolat* suggested the possibilities of chocolate confections flavoured with chilli, clients of ultra-traditional Valzani in Trastevere began asking for them. Happy to oblige, the *pasticceria* developed a recipe, now patented and secret, for a cocoa-covered tablet that tastes like a chocolate truffle – with a kick that arrives several seconds after the voluptuous filling starts to melt in the mouth. The name, "little devils", refers to the piquancy of the chilli.

ANTIPASTI

Fried courgette flowers, vinegar-spiked vegetables, or sliced cure

neats – the antipasto is probably the most variable course of the meal.

Nothing seems more typical of the Italian trattoria than a colourful antipasto buffet of marinated fish, grilled vegetables, slices of frittata, and various other savoury tidbits. Yet the antipasto course (the word means "before the meal") is not traditional in Rome, which is why rudimentary trattorias often offer nothing more than a plate of prosciutto, perhaps with melon or figs in summer. When paired with rustic Roman bread, most antipasti do double duty as snacks or lunch. Wherever you put them in the meal, a deep-fried *fiore di zucca* or a wedge of frittata spells Rome.

BRUSCHETTA AL POMODORO
Garlic-Rubbed Toast with Fresh Tomatoes and Basil

It seems, and is, so simple – garlic-rubbed toasted bread with raw tomato on top – but like many of the capital city's favourite foods, bruschetta al pomodoro *brings you face to face with the brilliance of basic Roman ingredients. The classic bread for bruschetta is* pane casereccio, *the ordinary Roman loaf, though good hand-sliced sourdough or country bread would also work well. If you can't find flavourful ripe tomatoes and fresh basil, use none at all, and make the bruschetta with just garlic, salt, and olive oil.*

1 The bread can be toasted under the grill, on a ridged cast iron grill pan, or in a toaster. If using the grill, preheat it; heat a grill pan.

2 If using firm tomatoes, core them, then cut into slices about 5 mm (¼ inch) thick. If the tomatoes are red and ripe, core and skin them, then cut into 1 cm (½ inch) dice. Cut cherry tomatoes in half. Tear larger basil leaves into a few pieces; leave smaller leaves whole.

3 Toast the slices of bread under the grill or on the hot grill pan, turning once, for about 4 minutes or until crisp and golden on both sides. Alternatively, toast the bread in a toaster. As soon as the bread is ready, rub the garlic cloves vigorously over one side of each slice. The rough surface of the bread will shred the garlic like a grater, leaving very little in your fingers.

4 Divide the bread slices, garlic side up, between 2 plates. Arrange the tomatoes in a single layer on the bread. If you are using cherry tomatoes, squash the halves, cut side down, into the bread. Sprinkle with salt and drizzle generously with the olive oil. Scatter the basil evenly on top. Serve immediately.

Serve with a fruity white wine such as Orvieto Classico.

1 large or 2 medium tomatoes, or about 16 cherry tomatoes

About 16 fresh basil leaves, torn into little pieces

4 slices coarse country bread, about 1 cm (½ inch) thick

2 cloves garlic, peeled and left whole

Salt

2–4 tablespoons extra virgin olive oil

Makes 2 servings

Breads of Rome

Most Romans will not pick up a fork without a full bread basket on the table. Nor can they finish the meal without bread, since mopping up the last bit of sauce, called *fare la scarpetta,* is standard practise in all but the most formal settings. Even the language divides foods into *pane,* "bread", and everything else, *companatico,* literally "what you put with bread".

Despite the arrival of designer bakeries that feature walnut- and olive-studded loaves, most Romans prefer the old-fashioned chewy *pagnotta,* a round loaf of *pane casereccio* (home-style bread) that can be white or brown and is the traditional choice for bruschetta. Bread baked in wood-fired ovens in the nearby towns of Genzano and Lariano is considered to be among the best in Italy.

Other common loaves are the saltless *tipo Terni,* the airy *napoletano,* and the soft, dense *pane di grano duro.* The basic roll is the hollow, domed *rosetta,* split for a *panino,* but the football-shaped *ciriola,* named for an eel that once swam in the Tiber, and the flat *ciabatta,* or "slipper" loaf, are always available.

ANTIPASTO BIS DI PEPERONI E MELANZANE

Grilled Sweet Peppers and Aubergine

All summer, Roman markets are filled with beautiful aubergines and peppers, brought in from nearby farms. The aubergines can be chubby and pale violet to white or sleek and near black. The sweet peppers are green, yellow, or red, and big – often weighing 500 g (1 lb 2 oz) or more each. This recipe pairs the two vegetables because they are well suited to barbecuing or grilling and make happy partners – served with good bread and perhaps slices of mozzarella di bufala *– at* terrazzo *parties, but don't hesitate to prepare them separately. Both vegetables also make excellent side dishes.*

FOR THE AUBERGINE

2 cloves garlic

About 15 g (½ oz) fresh flat-leaf parsley leaves

120 ml (4 fl oz) extra virgin olive oil, or more as needed

2 teaspoons red wine vinegar

1 medium-large aubergine, preferably light skinned and round, cut across into slices 1 cm (½ inch) thick

Salt, preferably freshly ground

½ teaspoon dried chilli flakes (optional)

FOR THE SWEET PEPPERS

3 red or yellow sweet peppers

2 tablespoons extra virgin olive oil

1 teaspoon chopped fresh oregano, flat-leaf parsley, or basil (optional)

Makes 6 servings

1 Prepare a barbecue fire or preheat the grill to high. Alternatively, heat a ridged cast iron grill pan.

2 Halve the garlic cloves lengthways and cut away any green shoots. On a cutting board, using a *mezzaluna* (two-handled curved chopping knife), finely chop the garlic and parsley together. (Alternatively, use a chef's knife or a small food processor.) Transfer to a bowl (or work directly in the processor bowl), add the olive oil and vinegar, and mix well. Set aside.

3 If barbecuing, when the coals are ready, lay the aubergine slices and whole peppers on the rack about 20 cm (8 inches) above the fire. Cook the aubergine slices for about 6 minutes or until tender, turning until both sides are marked with brown stripes. Barbecue the peppers, turning as needed, for about 10 minutes or until the skin is evenly charred and blistered on all sides and the flesh is soft. In both cases, the timing will depend on the intensity of the heat.

4 If using the grill, arrange the aubergine slices on the grill pan and grill about 15 cm (6 inches) from the heat, turning once, for about 4 minutes or until tender and lightly browned on both sides. Transfer the slices to a flat plate. Place the peppers on the grill pan and grill, turning as needed, for about 10 minutes or until the skin is evenly blistered and charred.

5 If using a ridged grill pan, chargrill the aubergine slices and peppers, in batches as necessary, following the timings for grilling.

6 At this point, the destiny of each vegetable diverges. Put the peppers into a paper bag, close the top, and set aside until cool enough to handle. Then remove them from the bag, cut off the stalk end and a thin slice from the base of each pepper, and pull off all the skin that comes away easily. Slit each pepper open lengthways and remove and discard the seeds. Using a small, sharp knife, peel away any remaining skin. Don't worry if some small patches won't come off. Cut lengthways into strips about 1 cm (½ inch) wide. As you work, cut away the ribs and flick away any tenacious seeds. Put the pepper strips in a small serving bowl and toss with the olive oil. Sprinkle with the herbs, if using, before serving.

7 Allow the aubergine slices to cool slightly. Select a straight-sided glass or ceramic serving dish just large enough to hold the slices tightly packed. Layer the slices in the dish, sprinkling each layer with the garlic and parsley dressing, a little salt, and a few chilli flakes, if using. If the aubergine seems dry, add more olive oil.

8 The peppers and aubergine can be covered and left at room temperature for up to 1 hour or kept in the fridge for up to 3 days. Bring the vegetables to room temperature before serving.

Serve with an aromatic white wine such as a Mueller-Thurgau from Alto Adige or a local Frascati Superiore.

SUPPLÌ AL TELEFONO

Rice Croquettes

The word supplì *supposedly derives from the French* surprise, *and refers to the core of molten mozzarella at the heart of this popular egg-shaped croquette, a ubiquitous appetiser in Roman pizzerias. Why* telefono? *When the* supplì *is bitten into and one half is pulled away from the other, the cheese forms a long string, which suggests, after a fashion, the cord linking the receiver and the base of a telephone. Despite the allusion, most Romans resist the temptation to make clever remarks about the city's sometimes "surprising" telephone service or the arrival of cordless technology.*

1 To make the tomato mixture, put the porcini in a small bowl, cover with warm water, and leave to soak for 15 minutes to rehydrate. Drain, squeezing out the excess liquid, and chop finely. In a frying pan over a moderate heat, warm the olive oil. Add the beef, onion, and mushrooms and sauté for 10 minutes or until the meat is no longer red. Stir in the tomato passata and salt. Bring to the boil, then reduce the heat to moderately low and simmer, uncovered, for about 20 minutes or until the sauce has reduced by about one-third. Remove from the heat and set aside to cool.

2 For the rice, bring a large saucepan of water to a rapid boil over a high heat. Add the salt and rice and cook, stirring occasionally with a wooden spoon, for 10–12 minutes or until the rice has softened but is still al dente. Drain the rice and spread it out on a large platter or baking tray to cool slightly. Add the eggs, butter, cheese, a pinch of salt, and the tomato mixture. Using your hands, mix well together. Leave to cool to room temperature.

3 To form the croquettes, whisk the egg in a small, shallow bowl until blended. Pour the breadcrumbs into a second shallow bowl. Using a soupspoon, scoop up some rice and form into a ball the size and shape of an egg. Using a forefinger, make an indentation in the side of the ball, insert a piece of the mozzarella deep into the centre, and close the rice around it. Roll

the ball in the beaten egg to coat evenly, then roll in the breadcrumbs, again coating evenly. Place the ball on a large, flat plate or tray. Repeat with the remaining rice and cheese, evenly coating each ball. When all the balls are formed, cover the plate and chill the balls for at least 1 hour or up to overnight before cooking.

4 Preheat the oven to its lowest setting and put an ovenproof platter in it. To cook the croquettes, pour olive oil to a depth of at least 5 cm (2 inches) into a heavy saucepan or deep, heavy frying pan. Heat to 165°C (325°F) on a deep-frying thermometer, or until a bit of rice dropped into the hot oil sizzles immediately on contact. Working in batches, fry the croquettes, turning as needed to colour evenly, for 5–7 minutes or until they are a deep sunburnt colour and have a crisp crust. Using a slotted spoon, transfer to kitchen paper to drain. Then place on the platter in the oven to keep warm while you fry the remaining croquettes.

5 Serve the croquettes while the mozzarella core is still hot. They may be eaten with a knife and fork, but for the traditional telephone-cord effect, they should be eaten from a paper napkin.

In Roman pizzerias, a light Castelli Romani is the typical partner, but an oaky Chardonnay from Friuli or elsewhere would be a good alternative.

FOR THE TOMATO MIXTURE

45 g (1½) dried porcini

1 tablespoon extra virgin olive oil

125 g (¼ lb) lean minced beef

1 small onion, finely chopped

440 ml (14 fl oz) tomato passata

½ teaspoon salt

FOR THE RICE

1 tablespoon salt, plus more as needed

440 g (14 oz) Arborio rice

2 medium eggs, lightly beaten

2 tablespoons unsalted butter

2 tablespoons freshly grated Parmesan

1 medium egg

125 g (4 oz) fine dry breadcrumbs

250 g (9 oz) fresh mozzarella, cut into rectangles the size and shape of large sugar cubes (about 24 pieces)

Olive oil, preferably extra virgin, for deep-frying

Makes about 24 croquettes

ZUCCHINE A SCAPECE
Marinated Courgette Slices

These simple marinated courgette slices, flavoured with a hint of mint, are constants of the antipasto selection in Rome's trattorias. The word scapece *may derive from the Spanish* escabeche *(pickling), a technique it resembles. Any courgettes will do for this dish, but the best are the beautiful* zucchine romanesche, *which have light green skin and ridges that make lovely star-like slices when cut across. They also contain relatively little water. Other courgettes will benefit from being cut several hours before frying and allowed to dry at room temperature on wire racks or tea towels to rid them of their extra water.*

2 cloves garlic

About 160 ml (5 fl oz) extra virgin olive oil

500 g (1 lb 2 oz) small or medium-sized, firm courgettes, trimmed and sliced 5 mm (¼ inch) thick

¼ teaspoon salt

1½–2 tablespoons red wine vinegar

About 10 fresh mint leaves, torn into pieces

Makes 4 small servings

1 Halve the garlic cloves lengthways, cut away any green shoots, and cut each half lengthways into 2 or 3 pieces. Set aside.

2 Pour the olive oil into a frying pan; it should be about 2.5 cm (1 inch) deep. Place the pan over a moderately high heat and heat until a courgette slice dropped into the oil sizzles on contact. Put a single layer of courgette slices in the pan and cook, turning once, for about 5 minutes or until well browned on both sides. As the courgette slices are ready, lift them out of the oil with a slotted spoon, give them a little shake, and put them in a small serving bowl. Continue frying the courgettes, adding them to the oil a batch at a time in order to maintain the temperature of the oil.

3 Sprinkle the courgettes lightly with salt, add the garlic, and stir in 1½ tablespoons vinegar, mixing well but gently. Add the mint leaves and stir once. Leave in the fridge or in a cool place for about 30 minutes or until the slices are no longer warm.

4 Taste and adjust the flavour with a little more vinegar, if needed. The courgette slices are delicate and delicious eaten straight away, but if you prefer them more tart, wait until the next day, after they have had a chance to marinate. Serve in the bowl.

Emphasize the southern character of the dish with a Campanian white wine, such as Fiano di Avellino or Greco di Tufo.

FIORI DI ZUCCA FRITTI IN PASTELLA

Fried Courgette Flowers with Mozzarella and Anchovies

Fiori di zucca, or "squash blossoms", are the male flowers of the courgette. The female flowers, which often remain attached to the courgettes sold in Roman markets, lack the distinguishing long stalks. The male flower is preferable here, but is often hard to find outside Italy. These bright orange blooms can be deep-fried, as in this dish, or added to delicate pasta sauces, risottos, or frittatas. Like many traditional Roman fried foods, this recipe, which calls for dipping the flowers in the simple batter known as pastella *before slipping them into hot oil, originated in the Ghetto, but today is prepared throughout the city.*

1 Cut off the stalk from each flower and remove the sharp, protruding points of the calyx at its base, then remove the pistils from inside, trying not to tear the flower. Rinse the flowers and dry gently with a tea towel or kitchen paper.

2 Place a piece of anchovy and a piece of cheese in the cavity of each flower and press the petals closed. If any flower is torn, just wrap its petals around the filling. (When fried, the batter will help hold the flower together.) Gently lay the stuffed flowers in a single layer on a plate.

3 Sift 150 g (10 oz) of the flour into a bowl. Add 310 ml (10 fl oz) water and mix with a fork until a thick batter forms. To test, dip your finger into the batter; it should coat it without dripping. Adjust the consistency by adding more flour or more water. Stir in ¼ teaspoon salt and the vinegar. Put the remaining flour in another bowl.

4 Preheat the oven to its lowest setting and put an ovenproof platter in it. Pour olive oil to a depth of 5 cm (2 inches) into a heavy saucepan or deep, heavy frying pan and heat to 165°C (325°F) on a deep-frying thermometer, or until a bit of batter dropped into the hot oil sizzles immediately on contact. Holding a stuffed flower by its base, dip it first into the flour, coating evenly and shaking off the excess, and then into the batter, coating generously. Lay the flower gently in the oil. Repeat, adding 2 or 3 more flowers and being careful not to crowd the pan. Deep-fry for about 5 minutes or until golden brown on all sides. Using a slotted spoon or tongs, transfer the flowers to kitchen paper to drain. Then place on the platter in the oven to keep warm. Repeat with the remaining stuffed flowers.

5 Sprinkle the fried flowers lightly with salt, then arrange on a warmed platter or individual plates. Serve at once.

Serve with a Castelli Romani white wine, such as Frascati or Marino, or emphasize the floral accents with a Gewürztraminer from Alto Adige.

12 courgette flowers

4 olive oil-packed anchovy fillets, each cut into 3 pieces

125 g (¼ lb) fresh mozzarella or *mozzarella di bufala* (page 105), cut into 12 pieces

470 g (15 oz) plain flour, plus more if needed

Salt

½ teaspoon white wine vinegar

Olive oil, preferably extra virgin, for deep-frying

Makes 4 servings

INSALATA DI FINOCCHIO
Fennel, Orange, and Olive Salad

According to Greek mythology, Prometheus stole fire from the gods on Mount Olympus and carried it to earth in a fennel stalk. The aromatic bulb has been a key player in Mediterranean cookery ever since. Fennel is a favourite winter vegetable in Rome, cooked or raw, but the addition of orange, recognized throughout Italy as fennel's natural partner, is of Sicilian origin. The small brownish-purple olives named for Gaeta, a picturesque port town in southern Lazio, are favourites in the capital for cooking and eating. This refreshing salad can go at either end of the meal, as an antipasto or a contorno.

2 rounded, rather than flat, fennel bulbs

1 blood orange or flavourful regular orange

Salt and white pepper

2 tablespoons extra virgin olive oil

About 24 Gaeta olives or other flavourful brine-cured black olives, pitted

Makes 4 servings

1 Trim off the stalks and fronds from the fennel bulbs and reserve for another use or discard. Remove the outer layer from the bulbs and cut away the tough core. Using a sharp knife, cut the bulbs lengthways into slices about 3 mm (⅛ inch) thick.

2 Using a sharp knife, cut a slice off both ends of the orange to reveal the flesh. Place the orange upright on the chopping board and, using the knife, cut downwards to remove the peel and pith, following the contour of the fruit. Cut the orange in half through the stalk end, then slice each half crossways as thinly as possible. Discard any pips and visible pith.

3 For many people the olives provide sufficient saltiness for this salad, but if you want to season it with salt you can do so this way: a few minutes before serving, place the fennel slices in a colander, sprinkle them with salt, and allow to drain off excess water before proceeding.

4 Divide the fennel slices among 4 plates. Lay the orange slices on top of the fennel, again dividing evenly, and drizzle the olive oil evenly over the top. Season with salt (if you haven't salted and drained the fennel) and white pepper, and scatter about 6 olives on each plate. Allow to stand for a few minutes before serving, to give the orange slices time to release some of their juice on to the fennel layer.

Serve with a dry white wine such as Pinot Grigio.

BRESAOLA CON RUGHETTA E SCAGLIE DI PARMIGIANO

Cured Beef with Rocket and Parmesan

Usually associated with the far north of Italy, bresaola, air-dried cured beef, is a fixture of the Roman Jewish table as a substitute for prosciutto and is popular today for its low fat content. Rocket, which Italians call rucola *and Romans call* rughetta *(or* ruchetta coltivata*), shares the stage with* rughetta selvatica *(page 45). Either will do in this recipe. Finally, Parmesan, an "import" from the Emilia-Romagna region, is as well rooted in Rome as elsewhere in Italy. This popular antipasto also makes a good summer main dish.*

1 If large, tear the rocket leaves into a bowl. Sprinkle with salt and the olive oil. Toss to mix well. Add a grinding of pepper if the rocket is mild; often its own peppery taste is sufficient.

2 Choose a white or light-coloured serving plate or individual plates that highlight the colours of the ingredients. Arrange the slices of *bresaola* around the edge of the platter or plates. Place the rocket in the middle. Using a cheese slicer or a vegetable peeler, shave the cheese over the rocket.

3 Sprinkle lightly with salt and freshly ground pepper and serve at once. Place the olive oil bottle on the table so everyone can add some to the *bresaola*. Serve with lemon wedges for squeezing over the top.

Serve with a sparkling wine such as a *metodo classico* or a sparkling Frascati.

---

60 g (2 oz) rocket leaves, any tough stalks removed, leaves rinsed and dried

Salt and freshly ground pepper

2 teaspoons extra virgin olive oil, plus more for serving

16 paper-thin slices *bresaola*, about 140 g (4½ oz) total weight

About 45-g (1½-oz) piece Parmesan

4 lemon wedges

Makes 4 servings

How to choose olive oil

A careful reading of the label is the first step to selecting a superior oil. The finest oils include a guarantee of provenance in the form of a *denominazione d'origine protetta* (DOP) or, more rarely, an *indicazione geografica protetta* (IGP), official quality designations that guarantee the origin of food products and agricultural products, respectively. To gain these highly respected stamps of excellence, producers within a geographical zone must meet the area's rigorous standards.

Top-quality extra virgin olive oils – the expensive estate-bottled kind that come in small, dark bottles with detailed information about growing and production conditions – should be used raw as a condiment. For sautéing and frying, use a good but less expensive extra virgin oil.

Although much of the extra virgin oil found in Roman kitchens comes from nearby Tuscany and Umbria, Lazio boasts two excellent DOP oils. Sabina DOP is produced in the Sabine Hills, in the provinces of Rieti and Rome, home to Europe's oldest producing olive trees. The other is fragrant, fruity Canino DOP, from the province of Viterbo.

FRITTATA DI ASPARAGI

Asparagus Frittata

The Italian frittata differs from the French omelette in that the latter is folded, with filling in the centre, while the former is flat, with the filling distributed evenly throughout. Some Romans like their frittata to be as thick as a quiche, while most others prefer it thin enough to slip between two slices of bread for a sandwich. This recipe yields a fairly thin frittata, but once you master turning it, you can try varying the amount of eggs to find the thickness you like best. Here, the filling uses the distinctive spring flavour of fresh asparagus. Other favourite fillings include courgettes, leeks, or artichoke hearts.

500 g (1 lb 2 oz) asparagus

2 tablespoons extra virgin olive oil, plus more as needed

4 medium eggs, at room temperature

3 tablespoons freshly grated Parmesan

Salt and freshly ground pepper

Makes 4 servings

1 Snap or trim off the tough end of each asparagus spear. Cut off the tips and set aside. If the skin seems tough, peel the bottom one-third or so of each stalk with a vegetable peeler. Cut the stalks on the diagonal into slices about 1 cm (½ inch) thick. If the tips are more than 2.5 cm (1 inch) long, cut them in half on the diagonal.

2 In a 25-cm (10-inch) non-stick frying pan over a moderate heat, warm 1 tablespoon of the olive oil. Add the sliced asparagus stalks and sauté for about 2 minutes. Add 1 tablespoon water, reduce the heat to low, and cover the pan. Cook until the asparagus slices are very tender. This will take just a few minutes. Using a slotted spoon, transfer the asparagus to a small bowl and set aside.

3 Return the pan to a moderate heat and add the remaining 1 tablespoon olive oil. Add the asparagus tips and cook, stirring, for about 5 minutes or until tender. If the pan seems dry, add a little more olive oil, then return the cooked asparagus stalks and toss all of the asparagus together for a few seconds. Reduce the heat to low and add a quick swirl of olive oil. Using a wooden spoon, spread the asparagus pieces evenly over the bottom of the pan.

4 In a small bowl, whisk the eggs until blended. Stir in the cheese. Add ¼ teaspoon salt and a few grinds of pepper and stir to mix.

5 Increase the heat under the pan to moderately low and pour in the egg mixture, being careful not to dislodge the asparagus. Cook gently, without poking or prodding, for about 15 minutes or until the egg mixture has set. If you are worried that the frittata may be sticking, once the edge has set, lift it with a plastic or wooden spatula to make sure the frittata moves freely. When the frittata has set and comes free from the pan, slide it carefully on to a flat dinner plate. Set the plate on one outstretched hand and invert the empty pan over it. Holding the pan and plate together, turn them over so that the frittata drops back into the pan, with the unbrowned side on the bottom. Remove the plate and return the pan briefly to a moderately low heat to brown the second side.

6 Slide the frittata on to a serving plate. Cut into wedges and serve warm or at room temperature.

Serve with a crisp white wine, such as a Sauvignon Blanc, from Lazio or elsewhere.

INSALATA DI MARE

Seafood Salad

The term insalata di mare *covers a broad range of dishes in Rome, from the standard trattoria jumble of squid rings and prawns to delicate compositions that change according to a chef's whim or the day's catch. This salad, inspired by a recipe from Al Presidente, one of Rome's premier fish restaurants, uses prized ingredients briefly cooked and laid gently on a bed of greens. It is lightly dressed to preserve the flavour of each element. If you have a bottle of prized aged balsamic vinegar on the shelf, add just a few drops at the end.*

1 If using prawns or langoustines, peel or cut away their body shells but leave their heads and tails intact. With a small, sharp knife, cut a shallow groove along the back and lift out and discard the dark vein. If using scallops, leave them whole. Pour water to a depth of about 5 cm (2 inches) into the bottom of a steamer and bring to the boil. Arrange the prawns, langoustines, and scallops on the steamer rack, cover, and steam for about 5 minutes or until the crustaceans turn pink and the scallops are just opaque throughout. Remove from the steamer and set aside while you finish cooking the remaining seafood.

2 If using cuttlefish, squid, or octopus, cut into bite-sized pieces, or leave whole if small. Bring a saucepan of water to the boil over a high heat. Squeeze a few drops of lemon juice over the shellfish, then cook in the boiling water for 2–3 minutes or just until tender. Drain and set aside.

3 Arrange a bed of greens on individual plates or a single large platter. Sprinkle lightly with salt and drizzle with a little of the olive oil. Arrange the seafood on the greens and garnish with 1 or 2 citrus slices for each serving. Drizzle lightly with the remaining olive oil. If using the balsamic vinegar, place just 1 drop on each of the white seafood pieces. Mix together the chives and parsley and sprinkle lightly on top. Serve at once.

Serve with a fruity white wine such as Greco di Tufo.

500 g (1 lb 2 oz) mixed shellfish, such as raw tiger or Mediterranean prawns, langoustines, shelled scallops, cleaned small cuttlefish, cleaned squid, and cleaned whole small octopus or octopus pieces, in any combination

½ lemon or lime

90 g (3 oz) lamb's lettuce or other mild salad greens

Salt

About 4 tablespoons finest extra virgin olive oil

TO GARNISH

Lemon, lime, or orange slices, or a combination

Best-quality balsamic vinegar (optional)

Finely chopped fresh chives and flat-leaf parsley

Makes 4 servings

Fish and shellfish

Long before Catholicism brought meat-less Fridays, Romans regularly sat down to fresh and preserved fish. Gourmets of the first century BC introduced fish farming, and during the empire fish were imported from the Black Sea.

In later centuries, Rome principally looked to the Tiber and the Tyrrhenian for its fish and shellfish, and some local waters still provide many of the city's favourites. Calamari or *totani* (squid) and *polpo* (octopus), in various sizes, are popular, as are *scampi* (langoustines), *gamberi* (prawns), *cozze* (mussels), and *vongole* (clams). Cooks turn to *orata* (gilthead bream) and *spigola* (sea bass), often farmed, as well as *rombo* (turbot) for simple white fish dishes. *Razza* (skate), known as *arzilla* in Rome, holds an honoured place in the local cooking, as do dark-fleshed fish, such as *sgombro* (mackerel) and fresh *alici* (anchovies).

Restaurants near the volcanic lakes to the north and south of Rome serve freshwater fish such as *persico* (perch). In the past, the Tiber yielded salmon, sturgeon, and small eels, but nowadays only herons and cormorants fish for their dinner there.

LA TIELLA DI GAETA CON LE CIPOLLE
Onion and Herb Tart

Tiella is a southern Italian word for a baking tin and, by extension, its contents, often a savoury pie or tart. The town of Gaeta, near the border of Campania, has earned recognition for its tiella, *a particular kind of* torta salata *(savoury tart). Once a whole meal for the poor, today such dishes are fixtures of antipasto selections. The* tiella di Gaeta *comes in many forms, with, among other fillings, anchovies and tomatoes, escarole and salt cod, or, as here, onions and* scamorza *cheese. This recipe calls for a 30-cm (12-inch) cake tin, but the size and shape of the tin for this rustic dish is not crucial.*

FOR THE PASTRY

**10 g (⅔ oz) fresh yeast or
1¼ teaspoons dried yeast**

315 g (10 oz) plain flour

315 g (10 oz) semolina flour

½ teaspoon salt

2 tablespoons extra virgin olive oil

FOR THE FILLING

**3 tablespoons extra virgin olive
oil, plus more for brushing**

**4 large onions, about 375 g
(12 oz) total weight, thinly sliced**

Salt and freshly ground pepper

**250 g (8 oz) ricotta,
preferably fresh**

**185 g (6 oz) smoked *scamorza* or
other mild smoked cheese
such as Gouda, grated**

**1 tablespoon *each* finely chopped
fresh flat-leaf parsley,
marjoram, thyme, and sage**

3 medium eggs

Makes one 30-cm (12-inch) tart,
or 8 servings

1 To make the pastry dough, in a small bowl stir the yeast into 2 tablespoons lukewarm water. Allow to stand for about 3 minutes or until creamy.

2 On a large work surface, sift together the flours and salt into a mound, then make a well in the centre. Pour the yeast mixture, olive oil, and 4 tablespoons lukewarm water into the well. Using the fingers of one hand, swirl the liquid in a circular motion, gradually incorporating flour from the sides of the well. Slowly add 250 ml (8 fl oz) water to the well at the same time, and mix until all the ingredients are well combined and a rough dough has formed. Knead vigorously for about 10 minutes, stretching and pressing, and striking the dough against the work surface, until it is soft and smooth and comes away cleanly from your hands and the work surface. To check if the dough is sufficiently kneaded, cut off a piece. The cut surface should be pocked with small air holes.

3 Shape the dough into a ball. Lightly flour a large bowl, place the dough in it, and cover with a damp tea towel. Leave to rise in a warm place for about 1 hour or until the dough has doubled in volume.

4 Meanwhile, make the filling. In a large frying pan over a moderate heat, warm 2 tablespoons of the olive oil. Add the onions and sauté slowly, seasoning with a little salt and pepper. When the onions are just starting to brown, after about 8 minutes, remove the pan from the heat.

5 If using fresh ricotta, drain as described in step 1 on page 169. In a bowl, combine the ricotta and

scamorza cheeses and add the herbs, a pinch of salt, and a few grinds of pepper. Then add the eggs one at a time, mixing well with a wooden spoon after each addition until fully incorporated. Add the onions and their oil to the cheese mixture and mix well.

6 Preheat the oven to 190°C (375°F). Using olive oil grease a 30-cm (12-inch) round cake tin that has 5-cm (2-inch) sides (grease even if the tin is non-stick). Alternatively, grease a large baking tray.

7 Knock back the dough and turn it out on to a lightly floured work surface. Divide the dough into 2 pieces, one slightly larger than the other. Using a rolling pin or your fingers, stretch and press the larger piece into a round about 40 cm (16 inches) in diameter and 2 mm (1⁄16 inch) thick. Transfer the round to the tin and press it over the bottom and up the sides, leaving at least a 2.5–5 cm (1–2 inch) overhang. Fill with the onion and cheese mixture, spreading it evenly, and drizzle with the remaining 1 tablespoon olive oil. Roll out the remaining dough into a 30-cm (12-inch) round. Carefully lay it over the filling and trim to size with no overhang. Bring the overhang of the pastry case up over the top and press to seal.

8 Prick the top in several places with a fork and brush lightly with olive oil. Bake for 40–45 minutes or until golden brown and quite firm. Transfer to a wire rack and leave to cool. Serve at room temperature, cut into wedges.

Gaeta is near the border of Campania, so a Campanian white wine such as Fiano di Avellino is a good match.

PRIMI

A handful of greens, a few clams, or a sprinkling of cheese and peppe

...nd a toss in the pan turn plain pasta into a Roman *primo piatto.*

The first course in Rome is usually pasta, to which most Romans are addicted. Gnocchi and thick soups like *pasta e ceci* share the honoured status. A day that does not include a meal with a proper *primo* is starvation. The traditional repertoire, extending from the simplest sauce of cracked pepper and *pecorino romano* to the most labour-intensive ravioli, covers every taste and ingredient. A trattoria will almost always offer the popular local dishes – *pasta alla gricia, al pomodoro,* and *al ragù* – while in more sophisticated restaurants, the *primo* is a canvas for the chef's imagination.

PASTA E CECI

Pasta and Chick-pea Soup

The combination of pasta and pulses is a Roman perennial. Borlotti beans, lentils, and chick-peas mix and match happily with ditalini *(thimbles),* maltagliati *(egg pasta scraps),* quadrucci *(pasta squares), or, as in this recipe,* taglierini *(long flat noodles), broken into pieces. This dish became a Roman icon with the 1958 comic film* I soliti ignoti *(Big Deal on Madonna Street). In it, bungling burglars break through a wall, not to a pawn shop, as they expect, but to a kitchen, where they console themselves with a pot of* pasta e ceci. *This recipe is based on the version served at Ristorante Paris, in the heart of Trastevere.*

1 Pick over the chick-peas, discarding any grit or misshapen beans. Rinse well, then place in a large bowl and add the bicarbonate of soda, 1 tablespoon salt, and warm water to cover generously. Cover and leave to soak in the fridge overnight.

2 Drain the chick-peas and put them in a large saucepan. Add cold water to cover generously, 2 teaspoons salt, and 2 of the garlic cloves. Bring to the boil. Reduce the heat to moderately low (to maintain a gentle simmer) and cook, uncovered, for at least 1–2 hours or until tender; the timing will depend on the age of the chick-peas. Drain, reserving the cooking liquid; you should have at least 500 ml (16 fl oz).

3 While the chick-peas are cooking, in a small frying pan over a moderate heat, warm the olive oil. Add the remaining 4 garlic cloves and the rosemary and fry for about 2 minutes or until the garlic is golden brown. Pour the oil through a fine-mesh sieve held over a large saucepan; discard the garlic and rosemary. Add the tomatoes and their juice, the potatoes, 2 teaspoons salt, a few grinds of pepper, and the chilli to the pan, and place over a low heat. Cook slowly for about 15 minutes or until the potatoes are soft.

4 Using a slotted spoon, transfer the potatoes to a bowl and mash with a fork. Return the potatoes to the pan over a low heat and add the drained chickpeas with about 250 ml (8 fl oz) of their cooking liquid (or lightly salted tap water). Cook for about 30 minutes to blend the flavours. (The soup can be made up to this point, then covered and kept in the fridge for 2 days.)

5 If the soup is very dense, add more of the chick-pea cooking liquid or some lightly salted water to thin it to a good consistency. Then taste and adjust the seasoning with salt.

6 Meanwhile, bring a large pan of water to the boil. Add 1 tablespoon salt and the pasta and cook until still very al dente. Drain the pasta and add it to the soup. Cook, stirring to mix all the ingredients together, for a further 1–2 minutes.

7 Ladle the soup into a warmed tureen or soup plates, sprinkle with the parsley, and serve at once. Have a pepper mill and bottle of olive oil on the table.

Serve with an interesting Lazio blend such as Concento, made of Syrah and Cesanese.

500 g (1 lb 2 oz) dried chick-peas

1 tablespoon bicarbonate of soda

Salt and freshly ground pepper

6 cloves garlic, crushed

125 ml (4 fl oz) extra virgin olive oil, plus more for serving

2 tablespoons chopped fresh rosemary

1 can (440 g) plum tomatoes

2 waxy potatoes, peeled and cut lengthways into narrow wedges

1 small dried red chilli

250 g (8 oz) *taglierini,* broken into 5-cm (2-inch) pieces

1 tablespoon finely chopped fresh flat-leaf parsley

Makes 4 servings

LA VIGNAROLA

Stewed Spring Vegetables

In springtime, la vignarola *is a veritable cult food, when, for a few magic weeks, young, tender broad beans, sweet green peas, and locally grown globe artichokes are available simultaneously in the markets. Many Romans insist that the ingredients be cooked together, while others maintain the vegetables must keep their separate identities until near the end, as in this version. Some feel that broad beans without* guanciale *is sacrilege; others prefer the vegetarian version. Yet all agree that* la vignarola *fits in nearly anywhere in the meal, as a* primo, *a light main course, or a* contorno.

3 artichokes

1 kg (2¼ lb) young, tender broad beans in the pod

1 kg (2¼ lb) young, tender peas in the pod

60 g (2 oz) *guanciale* (page 101), pancetta, or prosciutto, cut into small strips (optional)

1 or 2 tablespoons extra virgin olive oil, plus more for serving

4 spring onions, thinly sliced

Salt and freshly ground pepper

Makes 4–6 servings

1 Prepare the artichokes as for Braised Whole Artichokes (page 159), omitting the garlic. Set aside. Pod the broad beans and peas and set them aside in separate bowls. If using larger, older broad beans, bring a pan of water to the boil, add the broad beans, and blanch for 20 seconds. Drain and allow to cool. Split open the skin of each bean along its edge and slip the bean from the skin. Discard the skins. If using small, new broad beans, leave the skins on.

2 If using *guanciale,* place in a saucepan over a moderate heat and cook, stirring occasionally, for 2–3 minutes or until it starts to brown and render some of its fat. If using pancetta or prosciutto, warm 1 tablespoon of the olive oil in the saucepan, then add the pancetta or prosciutto and cook as described for *guanciale.* Add half of the spring onions and cook, stirring, for about 10 minutes or until translucent. Add the broad beans and stir a couple of times, then add about 125 ml (4 fl oz) water, a pinch of salt, and a grind of pepper. Bring to the boil. Reduce the heat to low, cover, and cook for about 20 minutes or until the beans are just tender; the timing will depend on their size and age. Top up the water occasionally to keep a little liquid in the pan.

3 Meanwhile, in another saucepan over a moderately low heat, warm 1 tablespoon olive oil. Add the rest of the spring onions and sauté for about 10 minutes or until translucent. Stir in the peas, and add 125 ml (4 fl oz) water, a pinch of salt, and a grind of pepper.

Bring to the boil, then reduce the heat to low, cover, and cook for about 15 minutes or until the peas are just tender; the timing will depend on their size and age. Be careful not to overcook the peas to the point where they lose their lovely green colour.

4 When both the broad beans and peas are cooked, combine them and their cooking liquid in a single saucepan and set aside.

5 Cut the braised artichokes in half lengthways, then cut each half into 4 or 6 wedges and scrape away any sharp leaves or choke in the centre of each wedge. Chop the wedges coarsely and add them to the peas and broad beans.

6 Place the saucepan over a low heat, cover, and simmer for 10–15 minutes or until the vegetables are heated through. Uncover and drizzle with a little olive oil, then transfer to a warmed serving bowl or individual plates and serve at once. If you can wait, the vegetables are even better reheated the next day.

Serve with a white wine with good structure and some oak, such as Cervaro della Sala from Umbria.

CREMA DI ZUCCA CON GAMBERETTI

Pumpkin Soup with Prawns

Pumpkins are typically associated with northern Italy, where they are featured in risottos and tortelli di zucca *(stuffed pasta). But a handful of pumpkin and other squash varieties, such as the richly flavoured, dark green Marina di Chioggia, are sold at Rome's vegetable markets and have always played a quiet but consistent role in the traditional cuisine. This modern interpretation of an old-fashioned recipe is based on the version served at the elegant and creative restaurant Agata e Romeo in the Esquilino district.*

1 In a saucepan over a low heat, warm together the olive oil and shallots and cook, stirring occasionally, for about 10 minutes or until the shallots are translucent. Add the pumpkin, potato, bay leaf, a good pinch of salt, a couple of grinds of white pepper, and about 750 ml (24 fl oz) water, or as needed to cover. Raise the heat to moderately high, bring to a steady simmer, and cook, stirring occasionally, for about 30 minutes or until the pumpkin is very soft.

2 Remove and discard the bay leaf and allow the soup to cool slightly, then purée in a blender or food processor, working in batches if necessary. Return to the pan and reheat gently to serving temperature. Alternatively, purée in the pan with a hand-held stick blender. Taste and adjust the seasoning with salt.

3 For the garnish, in a small frying pan over a moderate heat, warm the olive oil. When it is hot, add the prawns and sauté quickly for about 2 minutes or just until they turn pink and are opaque. Season with a pinch of salt and the dill.

4 Ladle the soup into warmed soup plates. Garnish each serving with prawns and serve at once.

Romeo Caraccio at Agata e Romeo recommends serving this soup with a fine, full-bodied Chardonnay from Lazio or elsewhere.

1 tablespoon extra virgin olive oil

2 shallots, thinly sliced

500 g (1 lb 2 oz) small pumpkin, or butternut or acorn squash, peeled and cut into 2.5 cm (1 inch) dice (about 375 g/12 oz)

1 medium waxy potato, peeled and cut into 1 cm (½ inch) dice (about 75 g/2½ oz)

1 bay leaf

Salt and freshly ground white pepper

TO GARNISH

1 tablespoon extra virgin olive oil

12 medium raw prawns, about 170 g (5½ oz) total weight, peeled and deveined

Salt

1 teaspoon chopped fresh dill or wild fennel

Makes 4 servings

Fountains and water

Rome's most prized and characteristic urban amenity is its fountains, which may be sculpted magnificently and as big as a building, like the Trevi Fountain, or cast iron and small, like the many street-corner *fontanelle* (little fountains). Since antiquity, Rome has prided itself on its water. Unless it is marked *"non potabile"*, it's all drinkable and can be a lifesaver on a hot day.

The sophisticated ancient Roman system of aqueducts and fountains ran dry during the Middle Ages but was revived in the Renaissance. Today, the local water infuses everything with wholesome goodness, from the coffee served at the neighbourhood bars to most soups, which, like this one, often rely on water rather than stock.

For those who insist on *acqua minerale,* several locally bottled options are available. For centuries, the most famous local mineral water has been Fiuggi, from the mountains east of Rome. It is widely credited with dissolving kidney stones, including those of Michelangelo. Of the waters from springs along the Via Appia, the lightly fizzy Egeria is the most popular.

SPAGHETTI ALLA CARBONARA

Spaghetti with Eggs, Cured Pork, and Cheese

Dispute over the origin of this decidedly Roman dish never ends. Did the carbonari *(charcoal makers) invent it? Or was it American GIs looking for a way to use their bacon and egg rations? Or does the name describe the black, carbon-like flecks of pepper? Whatever the origin of this delicious dish, the key is the technique. Finding the precise point when the eggs, added raw to cooked spaghetti, are no longer liquid, but not yet fully cooked, makes this dish work.* Carbonara *lends itself to variation, too, with chilli flakes instead of black pepper, wild asparagus instead of cured pork, or a grating of white truffle from Alba.*

185 g (6 oz) *guanciale* **(page 101), pancetta, or streaky bacon, preferably in a single piece or in slices at least 6 mm (¼ inch) thick**

1 tablespoon extra virgin olive oil (optional)

Salt and freshly ground pepper

500 g (1 lb 2 oz) spaghetti

30 g (1 oz) *pecorino romano,* **freshly grated**

30 g (1 oz) Parmesan, freshly grated, plus more as needed

2 medium eggs, plus 1 medium egg yolk, at room temperature

Makes 4–6 servings

1 If using *guanciale* or pancetta, cut it into strips about 2 cm (¾ inch) long and 6 mm (¼ inch) thick. If using bacon, trim off any rind, then cut it into 2.5 cm (1 inch) pieces.

2 In a large frying pan combine the *guanciale* or other meat and olive oil. Set over a moderately low heat and cook for about 15 minutes or until much of the fat is rendered and the meat has browned a little. It should take on an appealing colour without becoming too crisp. Leave the meat and fat in the pan, off the heat, and cover to keep warm.

3 Bring a large pan of water (at least 4 litres/7 pints) to a rapid boil over a high heat. Add 1 tablespoon salt and the spaghetti and cook until al dente, according to the packet directions, stirring for the first minute of cooking and occasionally thereafter.

4 Meanwhile, in a bowl, mix together both of the cheeses. In another bowl, whisk together the whole eggs and egg yolk until well blended. Stir half the cheese mixture and several grinds of pepper into the eggs.

5 From this point on, timing and temperature are crucial. Put a large serving bowl in the sink and set a colander in the bowl. When the pasta is ready, pour it into the colander, so that its cooking water will warm the serving bowl. Lift the colander quickly out of the water and shake a couple of times. Toss the drained spaghetti into the pan with the *guanciale* and stir around to coat the pasta with the fat. Empty the hot water from the serving bowl, reserving 250 ml (8 fl oz) in a separate small bowl or jug. Transfer the pasta and *guanciale* to the warmed bowl. Using a wooden spoon, stir the egg mixture into the pasta, mixing vigorously to coat the pasta evenly. Add a splash of the reserved cooking water if the pasta seems a little dry. Add an extra handful of grated Parmesan if it seems too wet. If the eggs scramble, the bowl or the pasta was too hot. If the eggs are too runny, something was too cold. If the beaten eggs were at room temperature to start, the bowl warmed with hot water should provide just enough heat.

6 Divide the pasta among warmed bowls and serve at once, with the remaining cheese.

One regional classic deserves another: serve with a crisp, full-bodied white wine such as Frascati Superiore or Marino DOC.

RIGATONI CON GUANCIALE E CIPOLLA

Rigatoni with Guanciale and Onion

The Roman speciality spaghetti all'amatriciana, *with a simple sauce of* guanciale *or* pancetta, tomatoes, and pecorino romano, *has swept the globe in recent decades. Make the sauce in* bianco *(without tomatoes) and you have the original form of the dish, also known as* alla gricia. *Add a sweet red onion from the area of Tropea, in Calabria, and some green peppercorns and you have* cucina creativa – *in this case the inspiration of Angelo Troiani, co-owner (with his brothers) and chef of Ristorante Il Convivio, in the heart of old Rome.*

1 In a small frying pan combine the onion, vinegar, olive oil, sugar, and a pinch of salt. Set the pan over a low heat and cook, stirring occasionally, for about 5 minutes or until the onion wilts. Remove from the heat and set aside.

2 While the onion is cooking, in a large, deep frying pan over a moderately low heat, fry the *guanciale* or pancetta for about 15 minutes or until quite crisp. Remove the pan from the heat. Using a slotted spoon, remove half the *guanciale* pieces and set aside in a warm place. Add the cooked onion to the *guanciale* in the large pan and keep warm over the lowest heat.

3 Bring a large pan of water (at least 4 litres/7 pints) to a rapid boil over a high heat. Add 1 tablespoon salt and the pasta and cook until al dente, according to the packet directions, stirring for the first minute of cooking and occasionally thereafter. Drain the pasta, but not too dry, and add to the pan containing the *guanciale* and onion. Remove the pan from the heat and toss the pasta to coat thoroughly. Add the cheese and toss again.

4 Transfer the pasta to a warmed serving bowl and sprinkle the reserved *guanciale* on top together with about 4 grinds of pepper. Alternatively, divide the pasta among individual warmed plates and garnish each serving with a cluster of the reserved *guanciale* and a grind of pepper.

Serve with a full-bodied, tannic red such as a Chianti Classico or other Sangiovese-based wine.

1 red onion, julienned

4 tablespoons white wine vinegar

1 tablespoon extra virgin olive oil

1 teaspoon sugar

Salt and freshly ground green or black peppercorns

250 g (8 oz) *guanciale* (right) or pancetta, cut into slices at least 6 mm (¼ inch) thick

500 g (1 lb 2 oz) short pasta such as rigatoni or *mezzemaniche*

90 g (3 oz) *pecorino romano*, freshly grated

Makes 4–6 servings

Guanciale, pancetta, and prosciutto

In Lazio's agrarian past, it was easier to glean fat from a pig than from olives, and peasants and city dwellers alike typically used lard, not oil, for frying and baking. The memories of those early tastes are evoked in the use of various types of salt-cured and air-cured pork in *spaghetti alla carbonara, all'amatriciana,* and *alla gricia,* among other dishes.

The word *guanciale* is used for any cheek meat, but in central Italy its first meaning is cured hog's jowl, favoured by purists for its delicate, sweet flavour. Rubbed with salt and black or red pepper and aged for three months, the characteristic triangular cuts can be seen hanging in Rome's many *salumerie* (shops that sell cured meats). Pancetta (salt-cured bacon) is sold *arroto-lata* (rolled) or *tesa* (in a slab). Some cooks prefer leaner, more strongly flavoured pancetta to *guanciale,* especially for cooking with full-flavoured ingredients such as tomatoes.

Prosciutto (air-cured ham), whether the prized sweet Parma and San Daniele varieties, or salty, rustic *prosciutto di montagna,* is also suitable for cooking, particularly if you prefer a leaner cut.

PASTA CON I BROCCOLI

Pasta with Broccolo Romanesco

In Rome, the word broccoli, *or its singular,* broccolo, *is used loosely for at least five different members of the Brassica family, all of which play major roles in the local diet throughout the colder months:* broccoli siciliani *(calabrese broccoli),* cavolfiore *(cauliflower),* cavolo broccolo *(a green cauliflower, which is properly called brocco-flower, but most people just describe it, rather than try to name it),* broccoletti *(sprouting broccoli), and* broccolo romanesco *(a green cauliflower with pointed florets). This recipe calls for the last, but works equally well with any of them.*

1 large *broccolo romanesco* or cauliflower, about 1 kg (2¼ lb), or calabrese broccoli or sprouting broccoli

Salt

2 tablespoons extra virgin olive oil, plus more for serving

1 clove garlic, crushed

1 small dried red chilli

6 olive oil-packed anchovy fillets

500 g (1 lb 2 oz) penne, rigatoni, or *conchiglie*

Makes 4–6 servings

1 Discard only the largest or any discoloured leaves from the vegetable. For *broccolo romanesco* or cauliflower, remove the core and separate the florets. For calabrese, separate the florets. Cut off the bottom of the thinner, more tender stalks and cut into 2.5-cm (1-inch) pieces. Cut off the bottom of the thicker stalks, then use a vegetable peeler or small knife to peel away the tough outer skin. Cut the thicker stalks into 1-cm (½-inch) pieces. For sprouting broccoli, discard large leaves, then cut into 2.5-cm (1-inch) pieces.

2 Bring a large pan of water (at least 4 litres/7 pints) to a rapid boil over a high heat. Add 1 tablespoon salt and the *broccolo romanesco* or other vegetable and cook for about 8 minutes or until quite tender.

3 Using a slotted spoon, transfer the vegetables to a colander. Leave the water in the pan for cooking the pasta later.

4 In a large, deep frying pan over a moderate heat, warm the olive oil. Add the garlic and chilli and cook, stirring occasionally, for about 2 minutes or until the garlic is golden brown and the chilli is browned (do not allow the garlic to burn). Using a slotted spoon, remove and discard the garlic and chilli. Add the anchovies to the oil remaining in the pan and cook, pressing on them with a wooden spoon, until they dissolve into the oil. Add the boiled vegetables.

5 Meanwhile, bring the vegetable cooking water back to a rapid boil, then add the pasta and cook until al dente, according to the packet directions. Stir for the first minute of cooking and occasionally thereafter.

6 While the pasta cooks, sauté the vegetables gently, breaking up the pieces with a wooden spoon. When the pasta is about half done, stir a ladleful of the pasta water into the frying pan. Allow the water to evaporate, then stir in a second ladleful of water and again allow it to evaporate.

7 Drain the pasta, but not too dry, reserving about 250 ml (8 fl oz) of the cooking water. Add the pasta to the frying pan, remove from the heat, and toss the pasta and vegetables together until well combined. Add a bit of the reserved pasta cooking water if the pasta seems too dry.

8 Transfer the pasta to a warmed serving bowl or individual bowls. Top with a swirl of extra olive oil and serve at once.

Serve with a fruity white wine such as Frascati Superiore.

CONCHIGLIE ALLA CAPRESE

Pasta Shells with Mozzarella, Tomatoes, and Basil

The taste of summer in Rome is the taste of tomatoes and basil, and a favourite dish of locals is insalata caprese, layers of sliced tomatoes and mozzarella drizzled with olive oil and bedecked with fresh basil leaves. It was only a matter of time before this popular salad became a primo piatto *in the form of this pasta dish. Because it can be prepared ahead of time and served at room temperature, it solves the perennial problem of* terrazzo *or garden entertaining: how to attend to the cooking indoors without ignoring your guests outdoors.*

1 Cut the tomatoes in half through the stalk. Put them into a bowl and add the olive oil and one-third of the basil leaves. Toss to mix. Set aside at room temperature to allow the flavours to blend while you prepare the remaining ingredients.

2 Cut the mozzarella into 2-cm (¾-inch) cubes or coarsely shred it with your hands. Set aside.

3 Bring a large pan of water (at least 4 litres/7 pints) to a rapid boil over a high heat. Add 1 tablespoon salt and the pasta and cook until al dente, according to the packet directions, stirring for the first minute of cooking and occasionally thereafter.

4 Just before the pasta is ready, add ½ teaspoon salt and a few grinds of black pepper to the tomatoes. When the pasta is cooked, drain it, but not too dry, and put it into a serving bowl. Pour over the tomato mixture, add the anchovies, capers, olives, and a sprinkle of chilli flakes, if using, and mix well. Leave the pasta to cool for about 5 minutes, then stir in the mozzarella pieces. (The pasta should be cool enough so that the mozzarella does not melt.)

5 The dish can be made up to 2 hours in advance and kept at room temperature, never in the fridge. Spoon into individual bowls or on to plates, or serve in a large bowl as part of a buffet.

Serve with a crisp white wine such as a Sauvignon Blanc.

500 g (1 lb 2 oz) cherry or baby plum tomatoes

125 ml (4 fl oz) extra virgin olive oil

About 15 g (½ oz) fresh basil leaves, torn into pieces

250 g (8 oz) *mozzarella di bufala* (right)

Salt and freshly ground black pepper

500 g (1 lb 2 oz) *conchiglie* or other pasta shape

8 olive oil-packed anchovy fillets, coarsely chopped (optional)

1 tablespoon salted capers, well rinsed (optional)

155 g (5 oz) Gaeta or Kalamata olives, pitted, or 1 tablespoon black olive tapenade (optional)

Dried chilli flakes (optional)

Makes 4–6 servings

Mozzarella di bufala

Mozzarella di bufala is made by hand from the milk of the water buffalo. Each ball of smooth white cheese weighs about 500 g (1 lb 2 oz) and displays the characteristic scar where it was separated from the mass (*mozzare* means "to cut off"). The cheese is also sold in smaller balls and in *trecce* (plaits). The flavour is pronounced and the soft but resistant texture sublime, and when the mozzarella is sliced, beads of milk ooze from pores in the cut surface.

Look for *mozzarella di bufala campana DOP.* Most of it is produced in Campania, but part of the official zone lies in southern Lazio. Similar cheeses made from cow's milk are properly called *fior di latte,* though they are often dubbed simply mozzarella or *mozzarella fresca.*

Romans use a great deal of mozzarella, primarily choosing the more abundant *fior di latte,* partly for economy and partly because it gives off less liquid when it melts. Both kinds turn up on pizza, in *insalata caprese,* and in the traditional snack *mozzarella in carrozza,* a fried mozzarella sandwich.

FUSILLI CON I CARCIOFI

Fusilli with Artichokes

Imagine a place where the chill of winter is alleviated by the most beautiful light the world has ever seen and by the arrival in the markets of so many artichokes that you have to think up new ways to use them. Such is Rome. For this recipe, size and shape are not important – in fact, this is a good chance to use up some of the less beautiful specimens. The artichokes should be tender, however, so trim them aggressively of any tough, inedible parts before cooking, and use as much pasta water as you need to make them soft and creamy. If you have any leftovers, use them to make a frittata.

1 lemon, halved

8 baby artichokes or 4 large artichokes

2 tablespoons extra virgin olive oil, plus more for serving

1 clove garlic, crushed

Salt and freshly ground pepper

4 tablespoons dry white wine or water

500 g (1 lb 2 oz) fusilli, penne, *mezzemaniche,* or rigatoni

Makes 4–6 servings

1 Fill a bowl with water and squeeze the juice of the lemon into it. Working with one artichoke at a time, trim off the base of the stalk, then peel away the stalks's dark, tough, stringy outer layer. Remove all the tough outer leaves until you reach the pale, tender inner leaves. Holding a small, sharp knife in your dominant hand and the artichoke in your other hand, turn the artichoke against the blade, raising the knife with each turn, to carve a sphere. Artistic perfection is not very important, but removing the tough parts is. Then cut off any tough tops of the remaining leaves until only the tender edible portion remains. Cut the artichokes in half lengthways, then cut each half into wedges not more than 12 mm (½ inch) wide at the widest point. (If using baby artichokes, simply quarter them lengthways.) Scrape away the choke (the fibrous hairs surrounding the heart). As you finish trimming each artichoke, drop it into the bowl of lemon water to keep it from turning black.

2 In a large, deep frying pan over a moderate heat, warm the 2 tablespoons olive oil. Add the garlic and cook, stirring occasionally, for about 2 minutes or until it is a deep golden brown. Using a slotted spoon, remove and discard the garlic.

3 Meanwhile, bring a pan of water (at least 4 litres/ 7 pints) to a rapid boil over a high heat.

4 While the water is heating, add the artichokes to the frying pan, season with salt and pepper, and cook over a moderately high heat, stirring, for about 10 minutes or until starting to brown and soften.

Reduce the heat to very low, add the wine, cover, and cook the artichokes, stirring occasionally, for about 25 minutes or until they are quite tender.

5 After the artichokes have been cooking for about 15 minutes, add 1 tablespoon salt and the pasta to the boiling water. Cook the pasta until al dente, according to the packet directions, stirring for the first minute of cooking and occasionally thereafter.

6 When the pasta is about half cooked, uncover the artichokes and stir a ladleful of the pasta water into the frying pan. Allow it to evaporate, then stir in a second ladleful and again allow it to evaporate. Continue to add the water and evaporate it until the pasta is ready. At the same time, use a wooden spoon to break up the artichoke pieces. (If they are not tender enough to cut with a wooden spoon, add more pasta water and cover the pan until they soften.)

7 Drain the pasta, but not too dry, add it to the frying pan, and remove from the heat. Toss the pasta and artichokes together until well combined.

8 Divide the pasta among warmed bowls, top each with a swirl of olive oil, and serve at once.

Serve with a soft, fruity red wine such as a Cabernet Sauvignon from Lazio or elsewhere.

TONNARELLI CACIO E PEPE

Tonnarelli with Pecorino and Pepper

Pasta, grated cheese, and black pepper – sounds simple. Yet few dishes in the Roman repertoire are trickier to get right. First, there are two schools, dry and wet. The former expects a grainy consistency, the latter a creamy sauce. In each case you need a sure hand and superb ingredients. Tonnarelli are a kind of chewy, square-cut fresh spaghetti, typical of Roman cooking. The modern version is the direct descendant of maccheroni alla chitarra, pasta cut on a wire frame that recalls guitar strings. If you don't want to make tonnarelli at home, use 500 g (1 lb 2 oz) dried spaghetti alla chitarra or regular spaghetti.

1 To make the pasta, mound the flour on a work surface and make a well in the centre. Break the eggs into the well, then add ½ teaspoon salt and the olive oil. Using a fork or your fingers, and working in a circular motion, gradually incorporate the flour into the eggs until a rough dough forms. Lightly flouring the work surface as necessary, energetically knead the dough for at least 10 minutes or until it is smooth and elastic. Shape into a ball, place in a bowl, cover the bowl with cling film, and leave the dough to rest for at least 30 minutes or up to 2 hours.

2 Divide the dough into 4 equal pieces. Flatten one piece slightly with your palm; re-cover the remaining 3 pieces. Set the rollers of a hand-cranked pasta machine at the widest setting and pass the dough through the rollers. Flour the dough lightly if it seems to be sticking, and pass it through the same setting 2 more times. Adjust the rollers to the next narrower setting. Fold the dough into thirds, as you would a letter, and pass it through the rollers. Repeat once or twice, again flouring as needed to prevent sticking. Fold and roll 2 or 3 times through each successively narrower setting, stopping at the third to the last setting. Lay the finished sheet on a lightly floured surface. Repeat with the remaining 3 pieces.

3 Cut the pasta sheets into 30-cm (12-inch) lengths. Fit the machine with the narrowest cutter, and pass each sheet through to produce narrow, square-cut ribbons. Place on lightly floured tea towels and dust lightly with flour to prevent sticking. Fluff the pasta ribbons with your fingers frequently and keep them covered with a tea towel until ready to cook.

4 Bring a large pan of water (at least 4 litres/7 pints) to a rapid boil over a high heat. While the water is heating, begin making the sauce. Place the peppercorns in a small frying pan over a low heat and heat for about 5 minutes or until fragrant. Pour into a folded piece of greaseproof paper and crush with a heavy weight. The resulting pepper should be considerably coarser than what a pepper mill produces.

5 When the water is boiling, add 1 tablespoon salt and the pasta and stir briefly to prevent sticking. Cook just until the pasta comes to the surface but is not quite done (1–2 minutes for fresh pasta). While the pasta is cooking, put a ladleful of the cooking water and the olive oil into a large, deep frying pan. Add a small handful of the cheese and mix vigorously with a fork or whisk. When the pasta is ready, using a spaghetti fork or metal sieve, lift it from the water and add it to the frying pan. (If draining in a colander, reserve 375 ml/12 fl oz of the cooking water.)

6 Place the pan over a low heat. Gradually add the remaining cheese, the crushed pepper, and spoonfuls of the pasta water as needed to make a creamy sauce. Toss to coat the pasta thoroughly, stirring and tossing for about 3 minutes. Serve at once in warmed bowls.

Serve with a light, young red wine such as Cesanese.

FOR THE PASTA

470 g (15 oz) pasta flour or plain flour

4 medium eggs

Salt

1 teaspoon extra virgin olive oil

FOR THE SAUCE

2 teaspoons black peppercorns

Salt

1 tablespoon extra virgin olive oil

185 g (6 oz) *pecorino romano*, freshly grated

Makes 4–6 servings

SPAGHETTI ALLE VONGOLE VERACI

Spaghetti with Clams in Their Shells

In Rome, most "vongole veraci", characterised by variegated shells about 4 cm (1½ inches) wide and by two little "horns" (siphons), are actually farmed Japanese littleneck clams rather than the prized, and increasingly rare, native species. They are most commonly used in spaghetti alle vongole, *part of the pantheon of Roman pastas –* carbonara, cacio e pepe, *and* gricia *are others – whose sauces are created directly on the cooked pasta. That means the dish is easy to put together but hard to fake: timing, temperature, an experienced hand, and, especially, undivided attention make all the difference.*

1 kg (2¼ lb) clams in the shell, scrubbed

Salt

4 tablespoons extra virgin olive oil, plus more for finishing

2 cloves garlic, crushed

1 small dried red chilli

500 g (1 lb 2 oz) spaghetti

2 tablespoons finely chopped fresh flat-leaf parsley

Makes 4–6 servings

1 In a large bowl or the sink, soak the clams in salted water to cover for about 30 minutes. (Use this time to assemble what you will need for the recipe.) Discard any clams that rise to the surface, then drain, rinse well, and place in a large frying pan.

2 Bring a large pan of water (at least 4 litres/7 pints) to a rapid boil over a high heat.

3 In a large, deep frying pan over a moderate heat, warm the olive oil. Add the garlic and chilli and cook, stirring occasionally, for about 2 minutes or until the garlic is golden brown. Remove the pan from the heat and, using a slotted spoon, remove and discard the garlic and chilli. Set the pan with the oil aside.

4 When the pasta water is boiling, put the pan holding the clams over a high heat and cover it. Add 1 tablespoon salt and the pasta to the pan of boiling water and stir for the first minute of cooking; stir occasionally thereafter.

5 After the pasta has cooked for 2 minutes, uncover the clams and reduce the heat to moderately high. Cook the clams just until they open – only a couple of minutes (watch them carefully). As they open, use tongs to transfer them in their shells to the pan holding the flavoured olive oil. Be careful not to bring any water with them, and discard any clams that did not open. When all the clams are in the second pan, strain their cooking liquid through a fine-mesh sieve lined with muslin, holding the sieve over the clams (this second pan should still be off the heat).

6 When the pasta is 2–3 minutes from being al dente, scoop out about 250 ml (8 fl oz) of the pasta water and set it aside. Drain the pasta in a colander, but not too dry.

7 Return the pan holding the clams to a low heat, add the pasta, and toss well with the clams. Add 2 tablespoons or more of the pasta water and continue tossing for about 2 minutes or until the pasta is al dente and a small amount of creamy sauce has formed. Mix in the parsley and a swirl of olive oil.

8 Divide the pasta among warmed bowls. The sauce tends to sink to the bottom, so don't serve the first bowl. After filling the second and third bowls, return the first serving to the pan and mix it with the remaining pasta, which will have more sauce. Then serve. Set out extra plates for the empty shells.

Pour a chilled dry white wine that evokes a day at one of Lazio's beaches: Tarquinia DOC or Cerveteri DOC.

FETTUCCINE AL RAGÙ

Fettuccine with Meat Sauce

This easy to make meat sauce is comfort food, typical of the Roman trattoria, where, especially on Thursdays, it is also used to sauce gnocchi. The ragù of Rome contains more tomatoes than meat, which distinguishes it from the more famous ragù of Bologna. Nor should the robust fettuccine of Rome be confused with the near-transparent tagliatelle from Emilia-Romagna. While technically a primo piatto, by today's standards a hearty bowl of fettuccine al ragù makes a piatto unico, or one-dish meal.

1 If making the pasta, prepare the dough and roll out as directed in steps 1 and 2 (page 109), but pass it through the next to last roller setting. Then, in step 3, fit the machine with the widest cutter and pass each sheet through the cutter, yielding ribbons 5–10 mm (¼–½ inch) wide. Place on lightly floured tea towels and dust lightly with flour to prevent sticking.

2 In a large saucepan over a low heat, warm the olive oil. Add the celery, carrot, and onion and cook, stirring occasionally, for about 5 minutes or until softened but not browned. Add the beef, season with about ½ teaspoon salt and several grinds of pepper, and cook, breaking the meat up with a wooden spoon, for about 10 minutes or until the meat is no longer red.

3 Add the wine, increase the heat to high, and bring to the boil. Stir in the tomatoes, breaking them up with a wooden spoon. Add the bay leaf and bring back to the boil. Reduce the heat to moderate and simmer, uncovered, stirring occasionally, for about 1½ hours or until the sauce is dense and the flavours have blended. Discard the bay leaf. Taste and adjust the seasoning.

4 Bring a large pan of water (at least 4 litres/7 pints) to a rapid boil. Add 1 tablespoon salt and the pasta. Cook the fresh pasta for 2–3 minutes, stirring for the first minute of cooking, then drain.

5 Transfer the pasta to a warmed serving bowl, pour over the sauce, and mix well. Serve in warmed bowls or plates, with Parmesan to sprinkle on top.

Serve with a full-bodied red wine such as Merlot.

Pasta dough (page 109) or 500 g (1 lb 2 oz) fresh fettuccine

2 tablespoons extra virgin olive oil

1 celery stick, finely chopped

1 carrot, peeled and finely chopped

1 onion, finely chopped

250 g (½ lb) lean minced beef

Salt and freshly ground pepper

4 tablespoons dry white wine

2 cans (440 g each) plum tomatoes, with juice

1 bay leaf

Freshly grated Parmesan to serve

Makes 4–6 servings

Cooking pasta

Always start with good-quality pasta, whether it is home-made, ready-made fresh pasta, or a packet of Italian dried pasta. The Italian formula for how much water to use for cooking follows a simple equation: for each 100 grams pasta, use 1 litre water. This roughly translates to 7 pints water for each pound of pasta. Bring the water to a rolling boil over a high heat, then add plenty of coarse salt followed by the pasta. Stir it almost constantly for the first minute of cooking and occasionally thereafter. Do not add oil to the water; the pasta won't stick if you remember to stir.

The pasta is ready when it is al dente, ("to the tooth", or still chewy). Start checking dried pasta at least 2 minutes before the cooking time on the packet. Most fresh pasta cooks very quickly, in 5 minutes or less, and gnocchi are done as soon as they bob to the surface. If you plan to finish the pasta in the pan with the sauce, drain it sooner, since it will continue to cook slightly. Drain pasta gently, using a metal sieve for small shapes. If you are cooking long strands, lift them with a spaghetti fork, and for ravioli use a slotted spoon.

RAVIOLI DI PESCE CON POMODORINI

Fish Ravioli with Oven-Roasted Cherry Tomato Sauce

The most classic Roman ravioli are filled with ricotta cheese and fresh spinach or with meat (in which case they are called agnolotti*). But ravioli are perfect for experimentation with other fillings, such as game, pigeon, mushrooms, or various cheeses. You can also try other shapes. Instead of small half-moons, as here, make them circular or square. This recipe, inspired by a pasta served at Ristorante Al Presidente, near the Trevi Fountain, relies on the pure taste of the fish. For a deeper flavour in the sauce, roast the tomatoes for up to 3 hours in a lower oven.*

FOR THE SAUCE

250–315 g (8–10 oz) cherry tomatoes

2 tablespoons extra virgin olive oil

Salt and freshly ground black pepper

2 cloves garlic, chopped

250 ml (8 fl oz) fish stock

FOR THE FILLING

2 tablespoons extra virgin olive oil

1 leek or 2 spring onions, white part only, chopped

375 g (¾ lb) fish fillets, such as cod, red mullet, or monkfish, or lobster meat, cut into 2.5-cm (1-inch) pieces

Salt and ground white pepper

Pasta dough (page 109)

1 medium egg yolk, lightly beaten

Salt

Fresh basil leaves to garnish

Makes 4–6 servings

1 Preheat the oven to 180°C (350°F). Put the whole tomatoes in a single layer in a roasting tin. Drizzle with 1 tablespoon of the olive oil and sprinkle with salt and pepper. Roast the tomatoes for 45–50 minutes or until they are soft and shrivelled. Remove from the oven and set aside. (This can be done several days in advance; cover with olive oil and keep in the fridge.)

2 To make the filling, in a frying pan over a moderate heat, warm the olive oil. Add the leek and sauté for 3–5 minutes or until translucent. Add the fish, reduce the heat to moderate, and cook, turning the fish frequently, for 5–10 minutes or until opaque throughout. Add a couple of spoonfuls of water if the fish starts to stick, but the pan should be dry when the fish is ready. Season with salt and white pepper. Transfer the fish mixture to a food processor and pulse until it is coarsely chopped, stopping before it becomes a paste. Turn out on to a plate and leave to cool completely.

3 To finish the sauce, in a sauté pan over a moderately high heat, warm the remaining 1 tablespoon olive oil. Add the garlic and cook for 1–2 minutes or until golden. Add the fish stock and bring to the boil. Reduce the heat to moderate and continue cooking until the stock is reduced slightly. Add the roasted tomatoes and cook, stirring, for about 5 minutes or until the sauce begins to thicken. Taste and season with salt and black pepper. Set aside.

4 Meanwhile, prepare the pasta dough as directed in step 1 on page 109. Roll out the dough as described in step 2, but pass it through the narrowest roller setting. Spread the sheets out on a floured work surface. Using a 6–7.5 cm (2½–3 inch) round cutter or glass, cut out at least 28 discs for about 4 servings. Place 1 teaspoon of the fish filling in the centre of each disc. Brush the edges of the disc with the egg yolk and fold over in half, forming a half-moon. Press the edges together to seal. Repeat until all the fish is used up. As the ravioli are shaped, set them aside on floured tea towels or trays.

5 Return the sauce to a low heat. Bring a large pan of water (at least 4 litres/7 pints) to a rapid boil over a high heat. Add 1 tablespoon salt and the ravioli and stir briefly. When they come to the surface, after 1–2 minutes, use a slotted spoon to transfer them to the sauce. Reserve the pasta water. Gently turn the ravioli in the sauce to coat evenly. If the sauce seems too dry, dilute it with some of the reserved pasta water, adding it 1 tablespoon at a time. Transfer the ravioli to a warmed platter or individual plates. Spoon any additional sauce on top, garnish with basil leaves, and serve at once.

Serve with a first-class white wine with good structure and some oak, such as the Umbrian Chardonnay Cervaro della Sala.

PASTA AL FORNO

Baked Farfalle with Mushrooms, Prosciutto, and Peas

The Roman category pasta al forno, literally "baked pasta", includes cannelloni, lasagne, and a host of labour-intensive delicacies, some in a pastry case, called variously timballo, pasticcio, and timpano. But sometimes, as here, it is simply unpretentious baked pasta with a sauce. Pasta al forno is traditional for Sunday lunch in Rome. This combination of peas, prosciutto, and mushrooms in a salsa besciamella (béchamel) is also perfect comfort food for a winter night. Peas are among the only foods that Romans regularly buy frozen and use year round. When fresh, they never play second fiddle, as they do here.

1 Preheat the oven to 180°C (350°F). Oil or butter a baking dish with a 2-litre (3½-pint) capacity.

2 Cut off the ends of the mushroom stalks. Break the stalks off where they join the caps and set them aside. Unless the gills are very small and tight, scrape them out with a small knife. Brush the caps clean and lightly peel them if the skins are blemished. Cut each cap into 6 or 8 wedges, depending on size. Clean and chop the stalks.

3 In a large frying pan over a moderately low heat, warm 1 tablespoon of the olive oil. Add the shallots and sauté for about 4 minutes or just until they begin to colour. Stir in the prosciutto and cook for a further 1 minute. Using a slotted spoon, transfer the shallots and prosciutto to a bowl and set aside.

4 Add the remaining 1 tablespoon olive oil to the same pan over a moderate heat. Add the mushroom caps and stalks and sauté for about 8 minutes or until all the liquid they release evaporates and they start to brown. Sprinkle with a little salt. When the mushrooms are golden brown, return the prosciutto and shallots to the pan and mix in the peas. Cook for 2–3 minutes to blend the flavours. Remove from the heat and set aside.

5 Bring a large pan of water (at least 3 litres/5 pints) to a rapid boil over a high heat. While the water is heating, make the béchamel sauce. In a saucepan over a low heat, melt the butter. Add the flour and cook, stirring constantly, for about 2 minutes or until it starts to brown. Very gradually add the milk while stirring constantly, then cook over a moderate heat, continuing to stir, for about 10 minutes or until the sauce starts to boil and thicken. Stir in 1 teaspoon salt. Remove from the heat and add to the pea and mushroom mixture, mixing well.

7 When the pan of water is boiling, add 1 tablespoon salt and the pasta and stir for the first minute of cooking; stir occasionally thereafter. When the pasta is 1–2 minutes from being al dente, drain it, but not too dry. Stir the pasta into the sauce mixture in the frying pan. Mix in all but 30 g (1 oz) of the cheese. Spoon the pasta mixture into the prepared baking dish. Dust with the remaining cheese and dot with the butter. (The dish can be made up to this point, covered, and kept in the fridge for up to 2 days. Bring to room temperature before baking.)

8 Bake for about 15 minutes or until bubbling and golden brown. Serve piping hot, from the dish.

Serve with a full-bodied red wine such as a Sangiovese or Merlot from Lazio, Umbria, or Tuscany.

500 g (1 lb 2 oz) *cremini,* **portabellini or chestnut mushrooms**

2 tablespoons extra virgin olive oil

2 shallots or 1 small onion, thinly sliced

125 g (¼ lb) prosciutto or cooked ham, including some fat, very thinly sliced and then coarsely chopped

Salt and freshly ground pepper

250 g (8 oz) frozen peas

350 g (¾ lb) farfalle

FOR THE BÉCHAMEL SAUCE

60 g (2 oz) unsalted butter

45 g (1½ oz) plain flour

500 ml (16 fl oz) whole milk

Salt

125 g (4 oz) Parmesan, freshly grated

1 tablespoon unsalted butter, cut into small pieces

Makes 4–6 servings

GNOCCHI AL GORGONZOLA CON RADICCHIO

Potato Gnocchi with Gorgonzola and Radicchio

In Rome, Thursday is gnocchi day – although no law forbids making the soft potato dumplings any other time. They are usually topped with a simple tomato sauce or meat ragù (page 113), or else served with something fanciful, such as several cheeses or even fish. Gnocchi with Gorgonzola, a blue-veined cheese of Lombardy that dates back to the tenth century, is a delicious pairing seen often throughout Italy. The presence of radicchio provides a touch of colour and an element of bitterness. A potato ricer gives the potatoes the right fluffy consistency for making gnocchi.

FOR THE GNOCCHI

1 kg (2¼ lb) floury baking potatoes

2 tablespoons salt

315 g (10 oz) plain flour, plus more as needed

FOR THE SAUCE

185 g (6 oz) red radicchio leaves, coarsely shredded

1 tablespoon extra virgin olive oil

Salt and freshly ground pepper

125 g (¼ lb) *gorgonzola dolce*, cut into small pieces

4 tablespoons double cream

60 g (2 oz) Parmesan, freshly grated

1 tablespoon chopped fresh flat-leaf parsley (optional)

Makes 4–6 servings

1 To make the gnocchi, put the potatoes in a large saucepan and cover generously with cold water. Add the salt, then cover the pan, place it over a moderately high heat, and bring to the boil. Cook for about 30 minutes or until the potatoes are tender when pierced with the tip of a knife. Drain the potatoes and peel them while they are still hot. Immediately put them through a potato ricer, allowing them to fall in a mound on the clean work surface.

2 Using your hands, gradually incorporate the flour into the potatoes. Keep adding and mixing in the flour until you have a pliable dough that no longer sticks to your hands (add more flour as needed). When the dough is ready, pull or cut off small handfuls. Dusting your palms and the work surface with flour as necessary, roll each handful of dough back and forth on the surface to form a rope about 1 cm (½ inch) in diameter. Cut each rope crossways into 2 cm (¾ inch) pieces, then press each piece with the prongs of a fork, flouring the fork as necessary. As each piece is shaped, place it on a tray lined with a floured tea towel. The gnocchi should not touch one another.

4 To make the sauce, in a large, deep frying pan combine the radicchio, olive oil, and 2 tablespoons water. Sprinkle with salt and pepper. Set over a moderate heat and cook, stirring, for about 5 minutes or until the leaves have wilted. Add more water, 1 tablespoon at a time, if needed to keep the leaves from sticking to the pan. Using a slotted spoon, transfer the radicchio to a bowl and set aside. Reserve the frying pan.

5 Bring a large pan of water (at least 4 litres/7 pints) to a rapid boil over a high heat. When the water is boiling add 1 tablespoon salt.

6 Return the frying pan to a low heat, add the *gorgonzola dolce,* and stir with a wooden spoon until the cheese starts to melt. Add the cream and keep stirring. Return the radicchio to the pan.

7 Drop the gnocchi, a handful at a time, into the boiling water. Keep a careful eye on them, and as soon as they bob to the surface – after about 3 minutes – lift them out with a slotted spoon and drop them into the pan with the sauce. Stir gently in the sauce to coat. When all of the gnocchi are in the sauce, stir in the Parmesan and sprinkle with the parsley, if using.

8 Transfer the gnocchi to a warmed platter or individual plates and serve at once.

Serve with a fragrant, full-bodied white wine such as a Malvasia or Malvasia blend.

PIZZA CON PEPERONI, POMODORI, E ALICI

Pizza with Roasted Sweet Peppers, Tomatoes, and Anchovies

When Romans want to suggest a casual meal with new acquaintances, they say: "Let's have a pizza sometime". Every neighbourhood has at least one pizzeria, and the best have wood-burning ovens twice as hot as the average home oven, not to mention talented pizzaioli (pizza makers) who pull and twirl the balls of dough to the size of a plate and a thinness that ensures a crisp base. Much like ravioli, pizza is the perfect blank slate on which to experiment with different toppings: try wild mushrooms and various cheeses, or a combination of mozzarella and prosciutto or rocket in place of the topping here.

1 To make the dough, in a small bowl, stir the yeast into 2 tablespoons lukewarm water. Leave for about 3 minutes or until creamy.

2 On a large work surface, sift together the flours and salt into a mound, then make a well in the centre. Pour the yeast mixture, olive oil, and 4 table-spoons lukewarm water into the well. Using your fingers or a fork, swirl the liquid in a circular motion, gradually incorporating flour from the sides. Slowly add 250 ml (8 fl oz) lukewarm water to the well at the same time, until the ingredients are well combined and a rough dough has formed. Knead vigorously, stretching and pressing the dough on to the work surface, for about 10 minutes or until it is soft and smooth and comes away cleanly from your hands. To check if the dough is sufficiently kneaded, cut off a piece: the cut surface should be pocked with small air holes.

3 Cover the dough with a damp tea towel and leave to rest for 5 minutes. Then divide the dough into 4 balls, cover again, and allow to rise at room temperature for about 2 hours or until doubled in volume.

4 If using fresh tomatoes, preheat the oven to 180°C (350°F). Put the tomatoes in a single layer in a roasting tin. Drizzle with 2 tablespoons of the olive oil and sprinkle with salt and pepper. Roast for 45–50 minutes or until soft and shrivelled. Set aside.

5 Preheat the grill to high. Arrange the peppers in the grill pan and grill about 15 cm (6 inches) from the heat, turning as needed, for 10–15 minutes or until the skin is blistered and charred. Watch carefully to avoid burning their flesh. Put the peppers into a paper bag, close the top, and set aside until cool. Cut off the stalks and pull off the charred skins. Slit each pepper open lengthways, remove and discard the seeds and ribs, and cut lengthways into strips 1 cm (½ inch) wide. Set aside.

6 Place a pizza stone or unglazed tiles on the bottom shelf of the oven and preheat to its highest setting. Lightly flour the work surface. Place one of the dough balls on the work surface, leaving the others under the damp towel. Knock back and flatten into a disc. Turn the disc over, sprinkle with additional flour, and, using a rolling pin or your hands, roll out or stretch the dough into a 30-cm (12-inch) round, turning it over and dusting it regularly with flour as you work.

7 Sprinkle a baker's peel or baking sheet with semolina flour. Gently lay the dough round on top. Cover evenly with one-quarter of the tomatoes or passata and drizzle with 1 tablespoon of the remaining olive oil. Slide the pizza on to the baking stone or tiles and bake for about 5 minutes or until the base begins to brown. Scatter one-quarter of the mozzarella and pepper strips over the top and add 3 anchovy fillets. Bake for a further 5 minutes or until the cheese has melted and the pizza base is browned and crisp. Begin assembling the other 3 pizzas while the first one is baking.

8 Remove from the oven and serve at once. Bake the remaining pizzas in the same way.

Serve with a young local Merlot.

FOR THE DOUGH

1¼ teaspoons dried yeast

315 g (10 oz) strong flour

315 g (10 oz) semolina flour, plus extra as needed

½ teaspoon salt

2 tablespoons extra virgin olive oil

FOR THE TOPPING

500 g (1 lb 2 oz) cherry tomatoes, or 180 ml (6 fl oz) tomato passata

6 tablespoons extra virgin olive oil

Salt and freshly ground pepper

2 red sweet peppers

500 g (1 lb 2 oz) fresh mozzarella, shredded or sliced, well drained, and blotted dry

12 olive oil-packed anchovy fillets

Makes 4 servings, or four 30-cm (12-inch) pizzas

SECONDI

Fresh fish from the Tyrrhenian Sea, celery-scented oxtail, and succulent lamb

...perfumed with rosemary – the Roman main course is all about flavour.

How better to enhance the taste of a whole fish than to bake it with sliced potatoes? And what could be a tastier way to cook tender lamb than to gently stew it with fresh rosemary? Such thinking is how the meat or fish course of the Roman meal, the *secondo piatto,* acquired its reputation for simple cooking. But it's not all quite so basic. *Saltimbocca alla romana,* veal escalope pan-fried with sage and prosciutto, or stuffed courgettes, both perennial favourites, illustrate a slightly greater degree of complexity. You'll find plenty of hearty stews and pot roasts in the local repertoire, too.

SALTIMBOCCA ALLA ROMANA

Veal Escalope with Prosciutto and Sage

Saltimbocca means "jump in the mouth", so the dish can safely be presumed to be particularly tasty. Elsewhere in Italy, saltimbocca can mean other recipes, but qualified by alla romana it refers to thinly sliced veal, prosciutto, and fresh sage, a staple herb of the Roman garden. Some recipes call for folding the layered ingredients in half, while others shape them into neat little involtini (rolls). But the standard preparation, given here, is to secure the sage to the stacked veal and prosciutto with a cocktail stick.

1 Using a meat mallet, pound the veal escalopes to flatten them somewhat; they do not need to be paper thin. Trim the prosciutto slices so they are slightly shorter than the escalopes. Lay a slice of prosciutto on each escalope and top with a sage leaf. Secure the layers together with a wooden cocktail stick.

2 Spread the flour in a shallow dish. In a large frying pan over a moderate heat, melt the butter. Dust the escalopes very lightly and evenly with the flour, shaking off the excess. Cooking in batches, place the veal, prosciutto side down, in the melted butter and cook gently for about 1 minute. Turn the escalopes over and cook for another minute. Season with pepper; if the prosciutto being used is not very salty, season with salt as well. Reduce the heat to moderately low and cook for a further 4–5 minutes or until the veal is cooked through and is a light golden brown.

3 Transfer the veal to a warmed serving platter and cover loosely with aluminium foil to keep warm. When all the escalopes have been cooked and removed from the pan, increase the heat to moderately high, add the wine, and bring to the boil. Deglaze the pan, allowing most of the liquid to evaporate and scraping up any browned bits from the pan bottom. Pour the hot pan sauce over the veal and serve.

Serve with a rich, flavourful white wine, such as Fiano di Avellino.

12 veal escalopes, about 500 g (1 lb 2 oz) total weight, each about 6 mm (¼ inch) thick

12 very thin slices of prosciutto, about 125 g (¼ lb) total weight

12 fresh sage leaves

Plain flour for dusting

2 tablespoons unsalted butter

Salt and freshly ground pepper

125 ml (4 fl oz) dry white wine

Makes 4 servings

Herbs of Rome

In Rome, perfuming roasting meat with fresh *rosmarino* (rosemary) is considered so important that butchers typically provide a few sprigs of the herb for free. Even without the meat, roast potatoes are naked without fresh rosemary and garlic. Romans traditionally cook only with fresh herbs, with the exception of bay leaves, which are picked fresh from a pot on the terrace or a tree in the park and left to dry in the kitchen.

Roman cooking is not spicy, except for the occasional use of *pepperoncini*, (small dried red chillies). Herbs are usually used one per dish, or mixed only with parsley. This recipe calls for *salvia* (sage), a common ingredient in local cooking. If you ask a Roman greengrocer for mint, he'll enquire: "For artichokes or for tripe?" *La mentuccia,* known elsewhere as *nepitella* (calamint), gives *carciofi alla romana* their minty flavour, while *menta romana,* a kind of spearmint, is essential for *trippa alla romana* and little else.

Basil reigns in summer: it is a principal ingredient in *spaghetti con pomodoro e basilico* and favourite imports from other regions, such as *insalata caprese* and traditional *pesto alla genovese*.

PESCE AL FORNO CON LE PATATE

Baked Whole Fish with Sliced Potatoes

The Romans feel, quite reasonably, that if you have a nice fresh fish, you should honour it with a simple preparation and not make it look, or taste, like anything else. The absence of sauces and condiments takes a little getting used to, but the reward is the subtle flavour and texture of the fish. This recipe is basic, but leaves plenty of room for variation. Instead of onions and parsley, try garlic and rosemary or other herbs, or cherry or baby plum tomatoes and a bit of marjoram. Instead of a whole fish, use fillets. In Rome, this recipe is often made with orata *(gilthead bream),* spigola *(sea bass), or* dentice *(dentex).*

About 2 tablespoons extra virgin olive oil

750 g (1½ lb) floury potatoes, peeled and sliced crossways 3 mm (⅛ inch) thick

Salt and freshly ground pepper, preferably white

1 or 2 whole fish such as sea bass, turbot, or cod, 1.25–1.5 kg (2¾–3¼ lb) total weight, cleaned with head and tail intact

1 sprig fresh flat-leaf parsley

4 lemon slices (optional)

4 onions, sliced

Finest extra virgin olive oil to serve

Makes 4 servings

1 Preheat the oven to 230°C (450°F). Brush a shallow baking dish as long as the fish (the fish can be laid diagonally) with some of the olive oil.

2 Spread the sliced potatoes over the bottom of the prepared baking dish, sprinkle them with salt, and drizzle them with a little more of the olive oil. Bake the potatoes, turning them over halfway through, for about 45 minutes or until they start to brown. As they bake, check them occasionally to make sure they are not sticking to the dish.

3 Meanwhile, rinse the fish inside and out and pat dry. Place the parsley and the lemon slices, if using, in the cavity and sprinkle with salt and pepper.

4 When the potatoes have started to brown, remove the baking dish from the oven and reduce the temperature to 120°C (250°F). Using a slotted spatula, move the potatoes to the sides of the dish to make room for the fish. Scatter the onion slices among the potatoes and set the fish in the centre. Drizzle more olive oil over everything. Return to the oven and bake

until the fish is opaque throughout when tested with a fork. This will take about 1 hour if using one large fish and 30–45 minutes if using 2 smaller fish.

5 Transfer the fish and vegetables to a platter. Fillet the fish and divide evenly among warmed plates, adding some of the potatoes and onions. Offer the head(s) to anyone who wishes to pick at the delicate meat. Have an olive oil bottle on the table.

To highlight the delicate flavour of the fish, serve an unoaked Chardonnay or a Frascati Superiore.

PETTI DI POLLO IN PADELLA

Pan-fried Chicken Breasts with Herbs

Boneless chicken breasts, which Roman butchers obligingly slice for their customers, are a favourite quick-cooking standby of the city's home cooks – a sprig of rosemary (which the butcher will provide free), a splash of wine, and dinner is ready. This dish, however, requires some advance planning, as the chicken is marinated. The recipe also illustrates an important principle of Italian food: Italian sauces do not rely on elaborate stocks. If you don't have time to make the stock from scratch, don't worry as most Italian home cooks would not hesitate to use a stock cube.

1 To make the stock, in a saucepan combine the chicken wings, carrot, celery, onion, ½ teaspoon salt, a few grinds of pepper, and 500 ml (16 fl oz) water. Bring to the boil over a high heat, skimming off any foam that forms on the surface. Reduce the heat to moderate and leave to simmer, uncovered, for about 10 minutes or until reduced by about half. Remove from the heat, strain through a fine-mesh sieve, and allow to cool, then cover and keep in the fridge until needed. Just before using, lift off and discard any fat that has solidified on top.

2 While the stock is cooking, in a shallow plastic or glass container, combine the olive oil, vinegar, rosemary, bay leaf, ½ teaspoon salt, and a few grinds of pepper, mixing well.

3 Remove the small fillet from each chicken breast and save for another use. Add the breasts to the container and turn them to coat all over with the marinade. Cover and leave to marinate in the fridge for about 2 hours, turning occasionally.

4 In a frying pan over a moderately high heat, warm 1 tablespoon of the marinade. When it is hot, add the chicken breasts and brown for about 5 minutes on each side. Reduce the heat to moderate and continue cooking for about 5 minutes on each side or until the chicken breasts are opaque throughout when tested with the tip of a knife. If the breasts are quite thick, cover the pan and cook for a few more minutes.

5 Transfer the breasts to a chopping board and leave to rest for 2–3 minutes. Using a sharp knife, cut against the grain on the diagonal into slices about 12 mm (½ inch) thick. Transfer the slices to a platter.

6 Add the chicken stock to the pan and bring to the boil over a high heat. Allow the stock to reduce slightly, scraping up any browned bits on the bottom with a wooden spoon. Season to taste with salt and pepper, then spoon the reduced sauce over the chicken slices. Serve at once.

Serve with a Frascati Superiore or one of the IGT white wines from the Castelli Romani.

4 boneless, skinless chicken breasts

FOR THE STOCK

2 chicken wings

1 carrot

1 small celery stick

1 small onion

Salt and freshly ground black pepper

FOR THE MARINADE

60 ml (2 fl oz) extra virgin olive oil

1 tablespoon balsamic vinegar

1 tablespoon chopped fresh rosemary

1 bay leaf, crumbled

Salt and freshly ground black pepper

Makes 4 servings

BACCALÀ IN GUAZZETTO

Salt Cod with Raisins and Pine Nuts in Tomato Sauce

Italy has its fair share of recipes using salt cod, and Rome makes two principal contributions to the collection: this recipe, also called baccalà alla romana, *and batter-fried salt cod fillets, found in pizzerias as an antipasto alongside* fiori di zucca *and in the* fritto misto *of restaurants offering Roman Jewish specialities. This preparation, with raisins and pine nuts, is likely to have migrated north from Sicily. Like fresh fish, salt cod is a standby for meatless Fridays, and even today many food shops pre-soak the dried fish so their customers can buy it ready to cook on Friday morning.*

750 g (1½ lb) salt cod fillets

60 ml (2 fl oz) extra virgin olive oil

185 g (6 oz) onion, thinly sliced

2 tablespoons pine nuts

2 heaped tablespoons raisins, soaked in warm water for 10 minutes to soften, drained, and squeezed dry

375 ml (12 fl oz) tomato passata

Makes 4 servings

1 Rinse the salt cod well in running cold water, then place it in a large bowl with cold water to cover. Leave to soak in the fridge for 24 hours, changing the water 3 or 4 times. Drain the salt cod and pat dry. Cut each fillet lengthways down the middle, then cut crossways at intervals of 5–7.5 cm (2½–3 inches), removing any bones or bits of skin. Set aside.

2 In a large frying pan over a moderate heat, warm the olive oil. Add the onion and sauté for about 10 minutes or until golden brown. Add the cod and cook, turning as needed, for a further 8 minutes or until browned on both sides.

3 Add the pine nuts, raisins, and tomato passata to the pan, reduce the heat to low, and cover. Cook for about 20 minutes or until the fish is quite tender when pierced with a fork. (The dish can be prepared up to this point, cooled, covered, and kept in the fridge, then reheated gently the next day.)

4 Transfer the cod and its sauce to a warmed serving dish and serve at once.

Serve with a chilled Chardonnay – either local or from further south (such as Sicily).

STRACCETTI DI MANZO CON RUGHETTA

Sautéed Strips of Beef with Rocket

There is something decadent about this simple preparation of sautéed shredded steak, which became fashionable in the late 1980s, along with rughetta *(rocket). The fervour has now cooled, and both* straccetti *and* rughetta *have settled into a permanent spot in the trattoria repertoire. The name* straccetti, *"little rags", suggests a dish born in poverty, but it is actually made with the finest steak and flavoured with balsamic vinegar, the popular condiment that originates in the area around Modena in Emilia-Romagna.*

1 If you have bought unsliced steak, put the piece in the freezer for 20 minutes to make slicing easier, then use a sharp knife to slice the steak as thinly as possible. With your hands or a fork, and working with the grain, tear and shred the steak into bite-sized "rags". Place the steak in a bowl, add 4 tablespoons of the olive oil, and season with salt and pepper. Toss well, then leave to stand at room temperature for about 15 minutes. Meanwhile, make a bed of rocket on a platter or individual plates.

2 In a frying pan over a moderately high heat, warm the remaining 2 tablespoons olive oil. Add the mushrooms and sauté for about 10 minutes or until their liquid has evaporated. Transfer the mushrooms to a bowl and set aside.

3 Pour off about half of the olive oil from the bowl holding the steak, and place it in the frying pan. When the oil is hot, add the meat with the rest of its oil and sprinkle with salt and pepper. Cook, stirring constantly, for about 4 minutes or just until the meat is browned. Add the wine and the butter and cook for 3–4 minutes or until the liquid in the pan reduces by about half and thickens slightly. (The flour-coated butter will slightly thicken the pan juices into a sauce.) Return the mushrooms to the pan, reduce the heat to moderate, and cook for a further 1 minute. Remove from the heat and stir in the vinegar.

4 Spoon the steak and mushrooms and their juices over the rocket. Serve at once.

Serve with one of the Merlot-based Lazio IGT red wines.

500 g (1 lb 2 oz) lean steak, preferably sliced very thin, with the grain, by the butcher

6 tablespoons extra virgin olive oil

Salt and freshly ground pepper

60 g (2 oz) rocket, any tough stalks removed

185–215 g (6–7 oz) fresh porcini, portabellini, or chestnut mushrooms, or a combination, brushed clean, trimmed, and cut into small wedges

125 ml (4 fl oz) dry white wine

1 tablespoon unsalted butter rolled in plain flour

2 teaspoons balsamic vinegar

Makes 4–6 servings

Mushrooms

The Italian edible fungus kingdom is divided into two realms, cultivated and wild. Cultivated mushrooms are led by white button mushrooms, which Italians commonly refer to by their French name, *champignons.* They turn up sliced fresh on *pizza ai funghi* and are most typically cooked *trifolati,* sautéed with garlic and parsley. *Cremini,* similar-looking earthy brown mushrooms, are also found in Roman markets. Grey-brown floppy *pleurotus* mushrooms, called *pleos* in the markets of Rome but also known as *geloni,* are available both cultivated and wild and can replace white mushrooms.

The king of wild mushrooms is the stocky brown *porcino, Boletus edulis,* which is eaten fresh or dried. The best specimens are sautéed or baked with garlic and oil and served as a *secondo* or on fettuccine. Porcini are, however, outranked by the elegant, egg-shaped *ovoli.* In the past, these were so plentiful that people used them in frittatas. Today, pricey *ovoli,* considered too precious to cook, are sliced and served raw with thinly sliced celery, shaved Parmesan, and fine olive oil.

ARROSTINO DI MAIALE
Roast Pork with Herbs

It is a common misconception that porchetta *is a suckling pig. In Lazio,* porchetta *is a hog, roasted whole by a specialist* porchettaro. *It is often prepared with large quantities of herbs and sold by the slice with slabs of wonderful* pane casereccio, *the chewy local bread, at street stalls like the one opposite the Basilica of San Giovanni in Laterano. The best* porchetta *in Lazio comes from the town of Ariccia, just south of Rome, but just about every fair and festival in the region has a* porchetta *stall. This dainty rolled roast that you can make at home will evoke the aromas of the popular local speciality.*

800 g–1 kg (1¾–2¼ lb) boned pork shoulder, rolled and tied

1 clove garlic, cut lengthways into 6 slivers

2 tablespoons coarsely chopped fresh rosemary

2 tablespoons coarsely chopped fresh sage leaves

Salt and freshly ground pepper

1 tablespoon olive oil

8 waxy potatoes

Makes 4 servings

1 Preheat the oven to 230°C (450°F). Using a small, sharp knife, make 6 small, evenly spaced slits in the pork. Insert a sliver of garlic, a tiny cluster of rosemary and sage, and a pinch of salt into each slit. Rub the meat all over with the olive oil and grind some pepper on top. Put the pork on a rack in a roasting tin and place in the oven to roast.

2 Meanwhile, bring a pan of water to the boil over a high heat, add the potatoes, and parboil for 3 minutes. Drain and pat dry, then add the potatoes to the roasting tin, placing them around the pork.

3 When the meat starts to brown, after about 20 minutes, reduce the oven temperature to 180°C (350°F). Continue to roast for about 40 minutes or until the pork is very brown on the outside and cooked through. An instant-read thermometer inserted into the thickest part of the joint should register 74°C

(165°F). During roasting, turn the potatoes as needed so they brown well on all sides.

4 Transfer the pork to a carving board and leave to rest for 5–10 minutes, away from any draughts. Snip the strings and carve against the grain into slices 6 mm (¼ inch) thick. Divide the pork and potatoes among warmed individual plates and serve at once.

Serve with a flavourful young local red wine such as Cori DOC.

ABBACCHIO ALLA CACCIATORA

Lamb Stewed with Rosemary

The first Romans were shepherds, which means that lamb has been the favourite meat here for close to three thousand years, just as the local cheeses have long been made from sheep's milk. Nearly every trattoria offers abbacchio al forno *(roast baby lamb) or* scottadito *(tiny grilled cutlets). Traditionally, no part of the animal goes to waste, and even today butcher shops display lambs' heads and menus offer offal such as* coratella *(heart, liver, and lungs) and* animelle *(sweetbreads). This recipe is inspired by the version served at Ristorante Checchino dal 1887, in the Testaccio quarter.*

1 To make the marinade, in a bowl mix together the vinegar, garlic, rosemary, chilli, and salt. Put the lamb pieces in a shallow glass or plastic container and pour over the marinade. Mix well, then cover and leave to marinate in the fridge for at least 12 hours or up to 24 hours, stirring occasionally.

2 If using a salted anchovy, rinse it under cool water and trim off the dorsal fin, then open the fish out flat and remove the backbone. Rinse again under cool water and pat dry.

3 In a heavy frying pan over a moderately low heat, warm the olive oil. Add the anchovy fillets and, using a wooden spoon, mash them into the oil. Add the garlic and rosemary and cook for about 2 minutes or until the garlic begins to colour. Increase the heat to high and add the lamb. Sprinkle the lamb with salt and pepper and add the chillies, then cook for about 10 minutes to brown the lamb on all sides.

4 Pour in the wine and the vinegar, reduce the heat to low, and cover. Leave to simmer gently for about 40 minutes or until the lamb is cooked through.

5 Using a slotted spoon, transfer the lamb to a warmed serving dish. Increase the heat to high and boil the pan juices for a few minutes to reduce slightly. Using a slotted spoon, remove the rosemary, garlic, and chillies and discard. Pour the pan sauce over the lamb and serve at once.

Serve with a Rosso Lazio IGT made from local grapes, such as Cesanese.

FOR THE MARINADE

125 ml (4 fl oz) red wine vinegar

1 clove garlic, cut into several pieces

1 tablespoon coarsely chopped fresh rosemary

1 small dried red chilli

½ teaspoon salt

1 kg (2¼ lb) boneless lamb from the leg, cut into 2.5–4-cm (1–1½-inch) pieces

1 salted anchovy or 2 oil-packed anchovy fillets

3 tablespoons extra virgin olive oil

1 clove garlic, crushed

2 tablespoons coarsely chopped fresh rosemary

Salt and freshly ground pepper

2 small dried red chillies

125 ml (4 fl oz) dry white wine

125 ml (4 fl oz) red wine vinegar

Makes 4 servings

ZUCCHINE RIPIENE

Stuffed Courgettes

The colourful aubergines, peppers, and other vegetables of Rome are just begging to be hollowed out and stuffed with tasty fillings. Courgettes, usually filled with the same beef mixture used for polpette (meatballs), are served as a main course year round, but the dish is best made in summer with zucchine romanesche *(page 187). This recipe features a vegetarian filling, which includes raisins and pine nuts. An Italian hand tool called a* vuotazucchine *(courgette emptier) makes quick work of hollowing out the vegetable, but an apple corer will work just as well.*

FOR THE FILLING

6 slices coarse country bread, about 90 g (3 oz) total weight, crusts removed

1 tablespoon extra virgin olive oil

1 small onion, chopped

1 medium egg, lightly beaten

30 g (1 oz) *pecorino romano* or Parmesan, freshly grated

1 tablespoon finely chopped fresh flat-leaf parsley

Salt and freshly ground pepper

1 tablespoon pine nuts

1 tablespoon raisins, soaked in warm water for 10 minutes to soften, drained, and squeezed dry

4 unblemished courgettes, each at least 3 cm (1¼ inches) in diameter

2 tablespoons extra virgin olive oil

Salt and freshly ground pepper

1 can (440 g) plum tomatoes, with juice, or tomato passata

Makes 4 servings

1 To make the filling, put the bread in the bowl of a food processor and process until fine crumbs form. Leave the breadcrumbs in the processor. In a small frying pan over a moderate heat, warm the olive oil. Add the onion and sauté for about 8 minutes or until translucent. Add the onion and its oil to the breadcrumbs, together with the egg, cheese, parsley, ½ teaspoon salt, and a few grinds of pepper. Process briefly just to mix. Add the pine nuts and raisins and process again for a few seconds. Alternatively, if making by hand, tear the bread slices into soft crumbs and chop the pine nuts and raisins coarsely with a knife, then stir all the ingredients together in a bowl.

2 Top and tail each courgette, then cut across into pieces about 7.5 cm (3 inches) long. Using a corer or a small knife, bore a large hole through the middle of each piece. The wall of the resulting cylinder should be about 6 mm (¼ inch) thick. Using the small knife or a teaspoon, stuff the courgette pieces with the filling mixture.

3 Select a frying pan large enough to accommodate the courgette pieces in a single layer, add the olive oil, and place over a moderately high heat. When it is hot, add the courgette pieces, laying them on their sides, and sprinkle with salt and pepper. Sauté lightly, turning as needed, for about 15 minutes or until just browned on all sides. Add the tomatoes or the passata and about 4 tablespoons water. Cover and simmer for about 1 hour or until the courgettes are quite tender when pierced with the tip of a knife. Check several times to make sure the courgettes are not sticking; if the pan looks dry, add a little more water.

4 Transfer the courgettes to a serving dish and spoon over the sauce. Serve at room temperature.

Serve with a young red, such as the local Cesanese.

CODA ALLA VACCINARA

Stewed Oxtail with Tomatoes and Celery

Widely regarded as Rome's most typical meat dish, a robust oxtail stew is the embodiment of quinto quarto *cooking (right). There are many recipes for this classic dish, but everyone agrees that the stew must cook for hours and contain a good deal of celery. Most cooks blanch the oxtails before stewing them. Some use grated chocolate, while others add raisins and pine nuts. This dish tastes even better the next day, when the rich flavours have had time to blend. Save any extra sauce and serve over pasta.*

1 Bring a large pan of water to the boil over a high heat. Drop in the oxtail pieces. When the water returns to the boil, drain the oxtail and set aside. Finely chop the carrot, onion, and 1 celery stick. In a large flameproof casserole over a low heat, warm 2 tablespoons of the olive oil. Add the chopped carrot, onion, and celery and sauté for 8–10 minutes or until tender.

2 In a large frying pan over a moderately high heat, warm the remaining 3 tablespoons olive oil. Add the oxtail pieces, in batches if necessary, and brown for about 15 minutes, turning to colour well on all sides. As the pieces are browned, transfer them to the casserole with the vegetables. When all the oxtail is browned, sprinkle with salt. Return the casserole to a high heat, pour in the wine, and cook for about 10 minutes or until it has evaporated. Add the tomatoes and their juice, ½ teaspoon salt, and a few grinds of pepper. If the oxtail is not fully submerged, add some water. Reduce the heat to low and simmer for about 3 hours or until the meat is falling from the bone. Check the liquid level occasionally and top up with water mixed with tomato purée if needed.

3 Taste and adjust the seasoning with salt. Cut each remaining celery stick into 6 pieces and add to the casserole. Continue cooking over a low heat for a further 30 minutes or until the celery is tender. Remove from the heat and stir in the chocolate. Transfer the oxtail pieces to individual warmed shallow bowls and ladle some of the sauce over them.

Serve with a Barolo, from Piedmont, or a Sangiovese.

1.25–1.5 kg (2¾–3¼ lb) oxtail, in 5-cm (2-inch) pieces, trimmed of excess fat

1 carrot, peeled

1 onion

6 celery sticks, or more to taste

75 ml (2½ fl oz) extra virgin olive oil

Salt and freshly ground pepper

250 ml (8 fl oz) dry white wine

2 cans (440 g each) chopped plum tomatoes, with juice

1 teaspoon tomato purée, if needed

1 teaspoon grated bitter chocolate

Makes 4 servings

Quinto quarto

Anyone who is put off by offal can avoid it, of course, but it does constitute one of the basic food groups of the traditional Roman kitchen. In Italian, the name for what's left over after an animal carcass has been quartered is the *quinto quarto*, or "fifth quarter". The cooking of offal is still centred in the Testaccio area, where, in the late nineteenth and early twentieth centuries, workers at *il mattatoio* (the abbatoir), in Via di Monte Testaccio, used to receive the hides, tails, and organs of the animals as part of their pay. The local trattorias devised tasty recipes for the offal as well. Some trattorias, such as Checchino dal 1887, are still there today.

Coda alla vaccinara is considered the city's signature meat dish, but Romans also enjoy *trippa alla romana*, tripe cooked with tomato sauce and mint; and *rigatoni alla pagliata*, the intestines of a milk-fed lamb or calf, still filled with mother's milk, cooked in tomato sauce and tossed with pasta. *Animelle* (sweetbreads) and *rigaglie* (giblets) are popular, as are the heart, liver, and lungs, which together are known as *coratella*.

POLLO ALLA ROMANA CON I PEPERONI

Chicken with Tomatoes and Sweet Peppers

The verb insaporire *sums up an essential concept in Italian cooking. Best translated as "to let the flavour develop", it refers to a process in which the ingredients of a dish take on a bit of one another's taste. In this recipe, the chicken and sweet peppers are cooked separately and then come together at the end, when each absorbs something from the other, resulting in rich, yet distinctive flavours. This dish was often served on Ferragosto, 15th August, the main summer holiday. Ripe, sweet peppers were in season, and meat – even chicken – was considered an indulgence reserved for special occasions.*

1 chicken, about 1.5 kg (3¼ lb), cut into 8 serving pieces

60 ml (2 fl oz) extra virgin olive oil

60 g (2 oz) prosciutto, coarsely chopped

Salt and freshly ground pepper

125 ml (4 fl oz) dry white wine

1 can (440 g) chopped plum tomatoes with juice

2 cloves garlic, crushed

1 tablespoon chopped fresh marjoram

1 large red sweet pepper, seeded and cut lengthways into strips 1 cm (⅜ inch) wide

1 large yellow sweet pepper, seeded and cut lengthways into strips 1 cm (⅜ inch) wide

Makes 4 servings

1 Rinse the chicken pieces and pat dry. In a large frying pan over a low heat, warm 2 tablespoons of the olive oil. Add the prosciutto and sauté for about 3 minutes or until it starts to become crisp. Add the chicken pieces, increase the heat to moderately high, and brown for about 15 minutes, turning to colour all sides. Sprinkle the chicken with salt and pepper and add the wine to the pan. Cook for about 5 minutes or until the wine has evaporated. Add the tomatoes, 1 garlic clove, and the marjoram. Bring to the boil, then reduce the heat to moderate and simmer, uncovered, for 20 minutes or until the chicken is cooked.

2 Meanwhile, in another frying pan over a moderate heat, warm the remaining 2 tablespoons olive oil. Add the remaining garlic clove and cook, stirring occasionally, for about 2 minutes or until golden brown. Remove and discard the garlic clove. Add the pepper strips to the pan and cook, stirring often, for about 15 minutes or until they are tender. Remove the pan from the heat.

3 When the chicken is ready, mix the peppers, with all their pan juices, into the chicken. Reduce the heat to low and cook together gently for 5 minutes to blend the flavours.

4 Transfer the chicken and peppers to a warmed serving platter and serve at once.

A young but flavourful red wine is the perfect match, such as a Barbera, from Piedmont, or Cesanese or Olevano Romano from Lazio.

CONTORNI

Spicy sautéed greens, piquant sweet and sour onions, tender artichokes

's a pity to keep vegetables this good on the sidelines.

In a traditional Italian restaurant, the main dish arrives alone on the plate, so you need to order any vegetable side dish, or *contorno,* separately. Preparations for these dishes tend to be quick and simple, though some Roman classics, such as caramelised onions or braised artichokes, take a bit more care. Portions are often hearty, and for vegetarians or anyone eating light, the *contorno* can stand in for the meat course. It might be a salad or sautéed greens in winter, or flat, green romano beans slowly braised with ripe tomatoes in summer.

INSALATA ROSSA

"Red Salad" of Tomatoes, Carrots, and Red Onions

Italian menus often mirror the flag – the sauce is red, the pasta is white, and the salad is green. But when the pasta is dressed in green, the salad should be red. In the Roman summer, when the luxurious growth of basil on the city's balconies and terraces makes emerald pesto alla genovese a favourite pasta sauce, this bright red salad follows it nicely. The tomatoes are full of flavour, and sweet red Tropea onions from Calabria are available in the markets. Serve the salad with bread for soaking up the juices.

1 If using large tomatoes, core them, then cut them in half crossways and into wedges. If using medium tomatoes, core and cut into wedges through the stalk end. If using cherry or baby plum tomatoes, core and cut into halves or quarters (depending on the size) through the stalk end. Set the tomatoes aside.

2 Using a mandolin, the slicing blade of a food processor, or a hand-held slicer, cut the carrots into very thin rounds and place in a salad bowl.

3 Add the onion to the carrots, then season to taste with salt and pepper. Mix in vinegar to taste, if using, and then the olive oil. (In Italy, tomatoes tend to be quite acidic, and vinegar is not normally used. If your tomatoes have no bite at all, you will probably want to use a small amount, say ½–1 teaspoon.) Add the tomatoes and torn basil leaves and stir to mix.

4 Divide the salad among individual plates and serve. (The salad can be assembled an hour or so before serving, but in that case, add the salt and vinegar, if using, at the last moment and toss just before serving.)

2 large or 3 medium tomatoes, preferably well-flavoured and vine-ripened, or about 16 cherry or baby plum tomatoes

4 young, tender carrots

1 small red onion or 2 or 3 spring onions, white parts only, thinly sliced

Salt and freshly ground pepper

Balsamic or red wine vinegar (optional)

1 tablespoon extra virgin olive oil

A few fresh basil leaves, torn into pieces

Makes 4 servings

Tomatoes

While fresh tomatoes are available year round, most Romans buy them only in the height of summer, when the locally grown *pomodori* are in the city's markets, sometimes mixed with "imports" from Campania, Apulia, and Sicily. During the winter, Italians prefer to use canned or bottled tomatoes and tomato passata, rather than rely on the hothouse harvest for their sauces.

In warm weather, large red tomatoes, labelled *da riso* in the markets, are filled with rice, baked, and serve as a *primo piatto*. Local custom dictates that salad tomatoes be firm and a bit green. Bright red spherical tomatoes still on the stalk are favoured for sauces, as is the sweet, oval San Marzano, which is cultivated in the warm countryside south of Rome. The small, pumpkin-shaped Casalino, eaten very ripe, is superb cut in half or chunks and squashed on to bruschetta or tossed in pasta – always with fresh basil. Many varieties of *ciliegino* (cherry tomato), notably those from Pachino, in Sicily, and slightly larger tomatoes, sometimes sold still on the branch, turn up on pizza and pasta, next to baked fish, and in salads.

VERDURA STRASCINATA
Greens with Garlic and Chilli

Green leafy vegetables are an integral part of the Italian diet, especially in the winter, when spinach, broccoletti, and wild greens are at their best. Anything tender enough to be eaten raw can be tossed into a salad, and the rest is customarily boiled and treated in one of two ways: all'agro, dressed at the table with olive oil and a squeeze of lemon juice, or strascinata (literally, "dragged"), also referred to as ripassata in padella, sautéed with garlic and chilli. Only spinach is prepared differently: briefly steamed and served all'agro, with butter, or sautéed with raisins and pine nuts.

500 g (1 lb 2 oz) broccoletti or other leafy green vegetable

Salt

2 tablespoons extra virgin olive oil

2 cloves garlic, chopped

1 small dried red chilli, cut into pieces, or ½ teaspoon dried chilli flakes

Makes 4–6 servings

1 Pick over the greens carefully, discarding any yellow leaves. Trim away any tough stalks. Rinse well.

2 Bring a large pan of water to a rapid boil. Add 1 tablespoon salt and the greens and boil for 6–8 minutes or until the greens are tender. Using a slotted spoon or skimmer, lift the greens out of the water and set them gently in a colander. Do not press or squeeze them: they should stay fairly wet. (The cooking water, filtered to remove any residual grit, can be reserved for another use, such as soup.)

3 In a large frying pan over a moderately high heat, warm the olive oil. When it is hot, add the garlic and chilli and cook, stirring occasionally, for about 2 minutes. Add the boiled greens to the pan, reduce the heat to moderate, and sauté for 7–10 minutes or until all the water from the greens has evaporated.

4 Transfer the greens to a warmed serving dish and serve at once.

CIPOLLINE IN AGRODOLCE
Sweet and Sour Onions

Romans have had a taste for sweet and sour since ancient times, when honey, grape must, or sweet wine provided the sweet, and vinegar or garum (right) the sour. In traditional Roman cooking, wild boar or beef tongue may be cooked in agrodolce, as are occasionally red mullet and salt cod. These onions, cooked until golden brown and tender, are ubiquitous in Rome during the colder months. This recipe yields piquant onions that nicely complement the simply prepared meats that are so much a part of the Roman menu.

1 To peel the onions, cut off the root end and remove the papery skin and, if it is blemished, the outer layer. (Holding them under cold running water as you work helps prevent tears.) Alternatively, bring a pan of water to a rapid boil over a high heat. Add the onions and boil for 1 minute, then drain and immerse in cold water to cool. Cut off the root end from each onion, then squeeze the onion; it should slide from its skin. Cut away any tenacious skin at the top. Rinse to remove any residual skin or dirt.

2 Place the onions in a heavy saucepan or deep frying pan large enough to accommodate them in a single layer. Pour over the oil and add the sugar, ¼ teaspoon salt, the vinegar, white wine, and 125 ml (4 fl oz) water. Stir just to mix.

3 Place the pan over a moderate heat and bring to the boil. Reduce the heat to moderately low and simmer, uncovered, for about 1 hour or until much of the liquid has evaporated to leave a thick sauce. The onions should be quite tender and golden brown.

4 Transfer to a serving bowl and serve warm or at room temperature. The onions will keep nicely, tightly covered, in the fridge for a few days.

500 g (1 lb 2 oz) small, flat onions such as Cipolline or Borettana, or pearl or button onions

2 tablespoons extra virgin olive oil

60 g (2 oz) sugar

Salt

125 ml (4 fl oz) white wine vinegar

125 ml (4 fl oz) dry white wine

Makes 4 small servings

The ancient Roman kitchen

The ancient Roman diet was based on vegetables, fresh cheeses, whole grains, fruits, chicken and fish, olives and olive oil, plenty of herbs and spices, and wine – not a bad diet, all round. And yet, the Roman kitchen has endured centuries of bad press due to the exaggerated descriptions of some extravagant dinner parties, and to Pliny the Elder's careless remark, in the first century AD, that *garum,* a popular fish sauce of the time, was made from rotten fish.

In fact, the recipe called for curing small fish under salt and herbs – not unlike modern salted anchovies – for three weeks. The liquid that resulted was the *garum,* which proved so important to ancient Rome that fortunes were made in its manufacture, notably at Pompeii.

Aside from some common ingredients, no continuous line can be drawn between the cooking of antiquity and the Roman cuisine of today. But there are some coincidental similarities: sheets of dried dough were layered with cheese and other ingredients in a proto-lasagne, and grape must and vinegar were used as a sweet and sour flavouring.

INSALATA VERDE

Salad of Roman Greens

This green salad, a variation of misticanza *(page 44), which takes advantage of the edible wild greens of the countryside around Rome, is meant to be a refreshing palate cleanser before dessert. Use the wildest salad greens you can find, though their cultivated cousins will do in a pinch. Raperonzoli (ramsons), small white roots with leafy tops, which appear in Roman market stalls in the fall and winter, are popular additions. The dressing is mixed directly on the salad, never separately, and should consist of the best extra virgin olive oil and red wine vinegar you can find.*

200 g (6½ oz) tender wild or cultivated salad greens such as rocket, lamb's lettuce, radicchio, escarole, and watercress, in any combination

3 spring onions, white parts only, thinly sliced

Salt and freshly ground pepper

2 teaspoons red wine vinegar

2 tablespoons extra virgin olive oil

Makes 4 servings

1 Pick over the greens carefully, discarding any discoloured leaves. Trim away any tough stalks.

2 Put the spring onions in the bottom of a large salad bowl. Sprinkle with salt and pepper, and add the vinegar and then the oil. Mix vigorously with a fork.

3 Lay the greens on top of the onions and sprinkle with a little more salt. The salad can sit like this for an hour or so before serving.

4 Just before serving, toss the salad well, making sure to coat the leaves evenly with the oil. Add a little more olive oil if the leaves are not all lightly glistening, being careful not to add too much.

CARCIOFI ALLA ROMANA
Braised Whole Artichokes

This dish of braised artichokes – the standard-bearer of traditional Roman vegetables – is remarkable for three things: the mystique of the carciofo romanesco *(large Roman globe artichoke), the special way the artichoke is cut, and the distinctive mint-like* mentuccia *(Roman dialect for* nepitella, *or calamint in English). Unfortunately, not everyone has access to real Roman artichokes (or* mentuccia*). Just buy the most tender artichokes available and aggressively remove anything that isn't edible. A* carciofo alla romana *should have an almost buttery texture. The more olive oil you use, the better the dish will be.*

1 Fill a bowl with water and squeeze the juice of the lemon into it. Working with one artichoke at a time, trim off the base of the stalk, leaving at least 5 cm (2 inches) attached, then peel away the stalk's dark, stringy outer layer. Remove all the tough outer leaves until you reach the pale, tender inner leaves. Hold the artichoke in one hand and a small, sharp knife in the other. Rest the artichoke against the knife blade without pressing and turn the artichoke against the blade. Then cut about 12 mm (½ inch) off the top. (The process may seem wasteful, but what remains is the most tender, edible part.) As you finish trimming each artichoke, drop it into the lemon water.

2 On a cutting board, using a mezzaluna (a two-handled curved chopping knife), finely chop together the herb(s) and the garlic clove, if using. (Alternatively, use a chef's knife or a small food processor.) Transfer to a small bowl, add 2 tablespoons of the olive oil and ¼ teaspoon salt, and mix well.

3 If the artichokes are tender, spread the leaves apart with your fingers to expose the centre and pull out a bit of the choke to create a small cavity. If they are not tender, the easiest way to expose the centre is to push an apple corer deep into the middle of the artichoke to cut out a plug of central leaves and some of the choke. Alternatively, you can pry out the leaves and choke with a spoon.

4 Using a small spoon, put about 2 spoonfuls of the herb mixture into each artichoke; reserve the rest. Place the artichokes, stalk side up, in a heavy pan large enough to hold them snugly in a single layer and deep enough to accommodate the stalks. Sprinkle the remaining herb mixture over the artichokes, then drizzle over the remaining 2 tablespoons olive oil, or a little more. Place over a moderate heat and brown lightly on the base for about 5 minutes. Pour in the wine to a depth of not more than 12 mm (½ inch).

5 Cover the pan. When the liquid boils, turn the heat to low. Put a folded tea towel over the top of the pan, making sure to keep its edges away from the burner, and place the pan lid on the towel. This will absorb moisture so the artichokes will not taste boiled. Finally, place a weight on the lid to make the seal as tightly fitting as possible. Cook the artichokes until they are quite tender. This will take up to 40 minutes, depending on how young and tender they are. Check the level of the wine 2 or 3 times while they cook, and top up with a little more if the pan is dry.

6 When the artichokes are tender, uncover and boil to evaporate any remaining liquid. Allow the artichokes to continue cooking for a couple of minutes in the oil that remains in the pan. Transfer the artichokes to a serving plate and pour over any oil remaining in the pan. Serve warm or at room temperature.

½ **lemon**

4 **young, tender artichokes**

3 **tablespoons fresh** *nepitella* **(see above), peppermint, pennyroyal, or flat-leaf parsley leaves, or a combination**

1 **clove garlic (optional)**

4 **tablespoons extra virgin olive oil, or as needed**

Salt

About 125 ml (4 fl oz) dry white wine

Makes 4 servings

PUNTARELLE CON LA SALSA

Puntarelle with Anchovy Dressing

Only a few years ago, the word puntarelle *was practically unknown outside the Eternal City. Winter visitors to Rome returned home with tales of a fascinating salad of fresh bitter greens with anchovy dressing. Summer visitors never knew what they were talking about. Today, pale green* puntarelle, *a variety of Catalonian chicory, with long, spiky, dark leaves, are still available only in the colder months, but they are now well known throughout Italy. Out of season, some Romans pair other salad greens with the* salsa. *Crisp frisée is probably the best substitute when* puntarelle *are not available.*

1 head *puntarelle* or frisée

1 clove garlic

2 salted anchovies or
3 olive oil-packed anchovy fillets

1 teaspoon red wine vinegar

3 tablespoons extra virgin olive oil

Makes 4 servings

1 If using *puntarelle,* remove the leafy external stalks, then separate the inner stalks that have buds on top. Discard the tough lower part of each stalk. Cut off the buds and slit the lower part of the bud all round, to create a daisy effect. Peel away the outer fibres of the remaining stalk, then cut the stalk lengthways into 4 or 5 strips, each about 3 mm (⅛ inch) wide. Rinse well. Immerse the pieces in iced water for about 30 minutes or until they start to curl, then drain and dry well. If you are using frisée, tear the leaves into bite-sized pieces, rinse, and dry well. Place the greens in a salad bowl.

2 Cut the garlic clove in half lengthways and remove any green shoot, then coarsely chop. Place in a mortar and pestle and grind the garlic. If using anchovies packed in oil, add to the mortar. If using salted anchovies, rinse each fish under cool running water and trim off the dorsal fin, then open the fish out flat and remove the backbone. Rinse the fillets under cool water. Set one aside for another use, and add the remaining 3 fillets to the mortar. Pound the anchovy fillets and garlic to a rough paste. Mix in the vinegar and then the olive oil.

3 Just before serving, pour the contents of the mortar over the greens and toss to coat the leaves evenly. Serve at once.

FAGIOLI A CORALLO IN UMIDO

Romano Beans with Tomatoes

In Italian, fagioli *usually refers to beans removed from a pod, such as white cannellini beans, while* fagiolini *have an edible pod, such as green beans. Yet it seems to bother no one that the long, flat, completely edible romano beans used in this recipe go by both names,* fagioli a corallo *and* fagiolini a corallo, *with a slight preference for the former in the markets of Rome. Nor does anyone explain the* corallo, *which means "coral", though it may reflect the fact that the beans turn reddish when left to dry on the plant.*

1 In a saucepan large enough to hold the uncut beans, warm the olive oil over a moderately low heat. Add the spring onions and cook, stirring, for about 8 minutes or until translucent. Add the tomatoes and the chilli, if using, increase the heat to moderate, and simmer, stirring occasionally, for 10 minutes or until the tomatoes reduce slightly.

2 Stir in the beans and sprinkle with salt and a few grinds of pepper. Reduce the heat to low, cover, and cook for about 30 minutes or until the beans are very tender. Check frequently and add a spoonful or two of hot water if the sauce looks dry. (The dish can be prepared up to this point, cooled, covered, and kept in the fridge, then reheated gently the next day. It will taste even better the second day.)

3 Transfer the beans to a warmed serving dish and sprinkle with the parsley, if using. Serve at once.

1–2 tablespoons extra virgin olive oil

3 spring onions, white parts only, thinly sliced

250 g (½ lb) very ripe fresh tomatoes, skinned, seeded, and diced, or 1 can (440 g) chopped plum tomatoes, with juice

1 small dried red chilli (optional)

500 g (1 lb 2 oz) romano beans or runner beans, ends trimmed

Salt and freshly ground pepper

1 tablespoon finely chopped fresh flat-leaf parsley (optional)

Makes 6 servings

Pulses

Pulses have an important place on the Roman menu. *Pasta e ceci (page 93),* chick-peas combined with short pasta and a little tomato, is perhaps the most beloved dish in town. A pan of lentils, symbolizing coins, is traditionally served on New Year's Eve, while lentils mixed with an equal amount of rice or pasta makes a hearty soup the rest of the year. Dried or fresh *fagioli borlotti,* pretty red-freckled beans, star in *pasta e fagioli.* Their pink-marbled pods are a feature of markets in the summer, when the fresh beans are boiled and dressed with oil and vinegar and mixed with slices of red onion. White cannellini beans are cooked with pork rinds and tomatoes for hearty *fagioli con le cotiche.* Hard to find *cicerchia,* which looks like a squared-off, flattened chick-pea, is usually used for soup.

No one enjoys broad beans more than the Romans. Early in the season, when the beans are still very small and tender, they are podded at the table and popped into the mouth raw between bites of *pecorino romano.* Later in the year, they are simmered with *guanciale.*

DOLCI

In Rome, almost any event or time of day is right for serving something sweet

ike hazelnut *tozzetti*, crumbly fruit *crostata*, or rich, custardy *zuppa inglese*.

Ricotta, hazelnuts, pine nuts, wild strawberries, sour cherries – the ingredients in Rome's sweets often come from the nearby countryside. A bowl of fresh fruit is the usual close to a meal, though a slice of pineapple has supplanted it in recent years. Most creative restaurants offer a menu of tempting desserts, many of them chocolate, but it is more common to find traditional sweets such as *torta di ricotta* in a *pasticceria* or at home. Trattorias and classic restaurants typically rely on a few old favourites, such as a tiramisù or crème caramel.

FRAGOLE CON IL "MOUSSE" DI RICOTTA

Strawberries with Ricotta Mousse

In Rome, nothing evokes summer better than finishing a meal with a dish of fresh fragole (strawberries) or fragoline di bosco (wild strawberries). The best are from the town of Nemi, which sits on a picturesque rise above a lake of the same name, south-east of Rome. A scoop of crema (custard) gelato or a squeeze of lemon juice and spoonful of sugar are the usual accompaniments for the berries, but their partner in this recipe is a sweet and decadent mix of ricotta, mascarpone, and whipped cream.

1 If the ricotta is very fresh and still exuding clear liquid, spoon it into a colander or a piece of muslin and suspend over a bowl. Cover it and leave it to drain in the fridge until it is quite dry, which can take up to 24 hours. For a smoother texture, remove the ricotta from the fridge and force through a coarse-mesh sieve placed over a bowl. For a more rustic texture, use the drained ricotta as is.

2 In a large bowl, combine the ricotta, mascarpone, caster sugar, and rum. Using a rubber spatula, mix until well blended.

3 In another bowl, using a balloon whisk or hand-held electric mixer, whip the cream until soft peaks form. Using the spatula, gently fold the whipped cream into the ricotta mixture until blended.

4 Spoon the ricotta mixture into six 250-ml (8-fl oz) dessert bowls or glasses, dividing it evenly. Cover and chill for at least 2 hours or up to 24 hours to allow the flavours to blend.

5 About 1 hour before serving, put the strawberries in a bowl and stir in the icing sugar. Cover and keep in the fridge until serving.

6 To finish, stir the vinegar into the strawberries. Top the ricotta mousses with the berries and their juices, garnish with mint, and serve at once.

Bring out the fruit flavour with a chilled Brachetto d'Acqui.

FOR THE MOUSSE

500 g (1 lb 2 oz) fresh ricotta

250 g (8 oz) mascarpone

155 g (5 oz) caster sugar

4 tablespoons rum or brandy

250 ml (8 fl oz) double cream

500 g (1 lb 2 oz) strawberries, hulled and quartered lengthways

2 tablespoons icing sugar, sifted

1 teaspoon white wine or champagne vinegar

Fresh mint leaves to garnish

Makes 6–8 servings

Fruit

Fruit is a hallmark of Roman culinary life, as evidenced in the fruit bowl for dessert, the glass of juice at a bar, or even the *frullato* (fruit-flavoured milk shake) or fruit gelato at the *gelateria*.

When the bright orange *nespole* (medlars) and deep-red *ciliegie* (cherries) appear, spring is turning into summer. *Fichi* (figs), destined to be peeled and eaten with prosciutto, arrive with the first heat of June and make an encore in September. Big *cantalupo* or small *francesino* melons keep the prosciutto company in between. *Albicocche, pesche,* and *susine* (apricots, peaches, and plums) are plentiful at midsummer, but throughout the season Romans feast on wild and cultivated strawberries and sweet *cocomero* (watermelon).

When the brown-flecked Muscat grapes appear, summer is turning into autumn. Juicy *fichi d'India* (prickly pears) come up from the south, but *kaki* (persimmons) can grow in Roman gardens. Winter means *mele* (apples) from the north-east; *pere* (pears), often cooked in wine; and the prized *tarocchi,* sweet blood oranges from Calabria and Sicily.

TORTA DI RICOTTA
Ricotta Tart

Ricotta is made in part from whey, a by-product of cheese making. Because of this, it is not considered a true cheese, but instead a latticino, or dairy product. While cow's milk ricotta is the most common, and ricotta made from water buffalo's milk and goat's milk is found as well, rich, creamy ricotta romana, made from sheep's milk (page 181), is particularly prized by Roman cooks. It is a popular filling for such sweets as sfogliatelle (filled flaky pastry) and cannoli, and for tarts, such as this recipe adapted from a dessert made by Enrico Licata, the talented pastry chef at Ristorante La Piazzetta, just off Via Cavour.

FOR THE FILLING

750 g (1½ lb) ricotta, preferably fresh

185 g (6 oz) granulated sugar

1 teaspoon Strega or Sambuca liqueur, or light rum

45 g (1½ oz) plain dark chocolate, shaved with a knife

FOR THE PASTRY DOUGH

185 g (6 oz) unsalted butter, at room temperature, cut into 2-cm (¾-inch) pieces

220 g (7 oz) icing sugar, sifted

2 tablespoons clear honey

⅛ teaspoon pure vanilla extract

Grated zest of 1 lemon

Pinch of salt

3 medium egg yolks, plus 1 more yolk for brushing, lightly beaten

375 g (12 oz) soft-wheat flour, sifted

1 teaspoon baking powder

Makes one 28-cm (11-inch) tart, or 8 servings

1 If the ricotta is very fresh and still exuding clear liquid, follow the instructions in step 1 on page 169.

2 To make the pastry dough, in a bowl combine the butter, icing sugar, honey, vanilla extract, lemon zest, and salt. Using your fingers, quickly work the ingredients together just until mixed. Using a wooden spoon, quickly work in the 3 egg yolks. In a small bowl, whisk together the flour and baking powder. Gradually stir the flour mixture into the butter mixture. As soon as the ingredients come together, pat into a rough mass. Cover the bowl with cling film and chill the dough for at least 2 hours or up to 24 hours.

3 Work the dough briefly until smooth, then divide into 2 pieces, one slightly larger than the other. Form each piece into a disc, and return the smaller disc to the fridge. Place the larger disc on a lightly floured work surface and roll out into a round about 32 cm (12½ inches) in diameter and 6 mm (¼ inch) thick. If the dough becomes too soft, return it to the fridge to chill until firm. Drape the round over the rolling pin and carefully ease it into a 28-cm (11-inch) flan tin with a lift-out base, gently pressing the dough over the bottom and up the sides. Using the tip of a sharp knife, cut around the inside edge of the tin bottom, leaving just a circle of pastry at the bottom and freeing the dough on the sides. Gather the freed strip of dough and pat into a ball, then roll back and forth on the floured work surface to create a rope 12 mm–2 cm (½–¾ inch) in diameter and 88 cm (35 inches) long – the circumference of the tin. Lay

this rope around the inside edge of the tin, resting it on the pastry base. (The rope is used to form a shallow, decorative reinforced edge to the tart.) Press the prongs of a fork against the rope to make a ridged pattern, and prick the base in several places. Cover and chill.

4 Preheat the oven to 190°C (375°F). To make the filling, put the ricotta in a bowl and beat vigorously with a wooden spoon to soften. Add the sugar and beat well to combine, then set aside to rest for 5 minutes. Stir in the liqueur and chocolate. Spoon the filling into the tin on top of the pastry base and spread it evenly. Remove the smaller disc of dough from the fridge and divide into 10 balls. Using the same technique you used for rolling the rope for the edge of the tart, roll each ball into a rope 6–12 mm (¼–½ inch) wide and 28 cm (11 inches) long. Lay 5 ropes across the filling. Lay the remaining 5 ropes across the first ropes to create a lattice pattern. Cut off any excess dough and discard it. Brush the ropes with the remaining beaten egg yolk.

5 Bake the tart for 40–45 minutes or until the pastry is a deep golden brown and the filling has set. Transfer to a wire rack and leave to cool. Cut into wedges and serve at room temperature.

Serve with a dessert wine such as Moscato Passito di Pantelleria, from an island off Sicily.

TOZZETTI

Filbert Biscotti

Tozzetti take their name from tozzo, *"stale bread", an allusion to their crunchy, crumbly character. They belong to the Lazio tradition of home-made dry sweets, which also includes various biscotti made with milk and eaten for breakfast, or with wine, such as* ciambelline al vino *(page 61).* Tozzetti *are distinguished from Tuscany's almond-laced* cantucci *by the use of hazelnuts, an important product of northern Lazio. These biscotti are a staple of the city's pasticcerie, so only dedicated bakers make them at home today. Serve them with a sweet wine in late afternoon or after dinner or with morning coffee.*

1 Preheat the oven to 150°C (300°F). Spread the filberts in a single layer on a baking tray and roast, shaking the pan every 10 minutes, for 25–30 minutes or until the nuts darken and smell strongly nutty. Pour them on to a plate to cool. (There is no need to remove the skins.) Put one-third of the cooled nuts into a food processor and pulse to chop very finely (do not process to a powder). Set aside.

2 In a large bowl, whisk together the eggs and sugar until well blended. Stir in the melted butter. Add the finely chopped nuts and mix well. Add the flour and salt and mix well. Finally, add the whole filberts and stir to distribute them evenly. At this point, the dough will be very stiff.

3 Increase the heat to 180°C (350°F). Line a large baking tray or two smaller baking trays with baking parchment.

4 Transfer the dough to a floured work surface. Divide the dough into 4 pieces. Form each piece into a rectangle 2 cm (¾ inch) thick, 5 cm (2 inches) wide, and about 15 cm (6 inches) long, or as long as your longest palette knife. Using the palette knife, transfer the rectangles to the prepared baking tray(s), spacing them about 5 cm (2 inches) apart.

5 Bake the rectangles, watching to make sure the bases do not get too brown, for about 30 minutes or until the top of each is firm to the touch. Remove from the oven and, using the palette knife, transfer the rectangles to a cutting board. Let cool slightly, then use a large knife to cut each rectangle on the diagonal into slices 1.5 cm (⅝ inch) thick. Place the slices, cut side down, on the baking tray (if all the slices won't fit, bake them in 2 batches). Bake for a further 20–25 minutes or until the biscotti colour slightly and are quite firm.

6 Transfer the biscotti to a wire rack and leave to cool completely. They can be stored in an airtight container at room temperature for several weeks.

Dip the biscotti in a sweet Aleatico di Gradoli, their historic partner. Vin Santo, a more widely available sweet wine from Tuscany, is a good substitute.

315 g (10 oz) filberts

3 large eggs

375 g (12 oz) granulated sugar

90 g (3 oz) unsalted butter, melted and cooled

470 g (15 oz) plain flour

⅛ teaspoon salt

Makes about 4 dozen biscotti

ZUPPA INGLESE

Sponge Cake with Custard and Liqueur

Most lovers of Italian food know that the name of this popular dessert literally means "English soup", which it was supposedly given for its resemblance to trifle. However, few know that one of the traditional ingredients, alchermes – a bright red liqueur flavoured with herbs and spices, invented by Florentine monks – derives its name from the Arabic qirmiz, which is also the source of the English word crimson. The composition of zuppa inglese may vary, the only constants being sponge cake, custard, and alcohol, preferably some of it red. To save time and labour, you can use a bought sponge cake.

FOR THE SPONGE CAKE

4 large eggs, separated

90 g (3 oz) granulated sugar

Pinch of salt

45 g (1½ oz) soft-wheat flour

1 teaspoon baking powder

FOR THE CUSTARD

500 ml (16 fl oz) whole milk

1 large strip lemon zest

1 large egg plus 3 large egg yolks

90 g (3 oz) granulated sugar

45 g (1½ oz) plain flour

1 teaspoon Sambuca

4 tablespoons rum, or more to taste

60 ml (2 fl oz) *alchermes* (see above) or framboise

125 ml (4 fl oz) double cream

2 teaspoons icing sugar, sifted

About 2 teaspoons grated dark plain chocolate

Makes 4 servings

1 To make the sponge cake, preheat the oven to 190°C (375°F). Butter a 20-cm (8-inch) cake tin, dust with flour, and tap out the excess.

2 In a bowl, using a hand-held electric mixer, beat together the egg yolks and sugar for about 5 minutes or until thick and pale yellow. When the beaters are lifted, the mixture should make a ribbon trail on itself. In a large bowl, using the mixer with clean beaters, beat the egg whites until frothy. Add the salt and beat until firm peaks form.

3 In a small bowl, whisk together the flour and baking powder. Using a rubber spatula, gradually fold the flour mixture into the yolk mixture. Stir about one-third of the whites into the yolk mixture, then gently fold in the remaining whites just until no white streaks remain. Pour the mixture into the prepared tin.

4 Bake the cake for about 30 minutes or until a skewer inserted into the centre comes out clean. Transfer to a wire rack and cool for about 10 minutes, then turn the cake out on to the rack.

5 While the cake is baking, make the custard. In a heavy saucepan combine the milk and lemon zest. Set over a moderate heat and heat until small bubbles appear round the edge. Remove from the heat and allow to cool slightly, then remove and discard the lemon zest. In a bowl, whisk together the whole egg, egg yolks, and sugar until well blended. Whisk in the flour, a spoonful at a time, then continue whisking for about 5 minutes or until thick and pale

yellow. Slowly pour the hot milk into the egg mixture, stirring constantly. Pour the contents of the bowl back into the saucepan, place over a low heat, and heat gently, stirring constantly, for about 7 minutes or until the custard is thick enough to coat the back of the spoon. Remove from the heat and pour through a fine-mesh sieve into a bowl. Stir in the Sambuca. Leave to cool to room temperature, stirring from time to time to prevent a skin from forming.

6 To assemble, use a serrated knife to cut the cake into slices about 5 x 7.5 cm (2 x 3 inches) and 6 mm (¼ inch) thick. Line the bottom of four 250-ml (8-fl oz) glass dessert bowls with some of the cake slices. Sprinkle the cake with some of the rum. Spread about one-quarter of the custard over the cake slices. Top with another layer of cake slices and sprinkle with 2 tablespoons of the *alchermes*. Spread one-third of the remaining custard over the top. Repeat to make 2 more layers of cake, liqueur, and custard, then finish with a cake layer. Cover and chill for several hours, or preferably overnight, before serving.

7 In a bowl, combine the cream and icing sugar and, using a balloon whisk, whip until medium-stiff peaks form. Spoon the cream on top of each serving and sprinkle with the chocolate.

Follow this dessert with a glass of aged rum or Sambuca.

TORTA DELLA NONNA

Grandmother's Tart

This deceptively simple dessert – a rich, creamy custard filling topped with pine nuts, baked in a case of rich pasta frolla, *or shortcrust – has long been a fixture of the Roman trattoria menu. Delicate ivory* pinoli, *the seeds of the stone pine, native to the Mediterranean, are encased in hard, dark shells attached to the outside of the pine cones found in profusion in the* pineti *(pine woods) around the city. This recipe, which adds the finely grated zest of a lemon to the custard, is, like the* torta di ricotta *on page 170, inspired by the* dolci *of gifted* pasticciere *Enrico Licata at La Piazzetta.*

1 To make the pastry dough, in a bowl combine the butter, icing sugar, honey, vanilla extract, lemon zest, and salt. Using your fingers, quickly and lightly work the ingredients together just until mixed. Using a wooden spoon, quickly work in the egg yolks. In a small bowl, whisk together the flour and baking powder. Gradually stir the flour mixture into the butter mixture. As soon as the ingredients come together, pat into a rough mass. Cover the bowl with cling film and chill for at least 2 hours or up to 24 hours.

2 Work the dough briefly until it is smooth. On a lightly floured work surface, roll out the dough into a round about 28 cm (11 inches) in diameter and 6 mm (¼ inch) thick. If the dough becomes too soft, return it to the fridge to chill until firm. Drape the round over the rolling pin and carefully ease it into a 23-cm (9-inch) flan tin with a lift-out base, gently pressing it over the bottom and up the sides. Trim off any excess dough, using the scraps to patch any holes and build up the sides of the tart if needed. Cover with cling film and chill while you prepare the filling.

3 To make the filling, in a heavy saucepan combine the milk and 150 g (5 oz) of the sugar. Set over a moderately low heat and heat, stirring, until the sugar dissolves. Continue to heat until bubbles appear round the edge. Remove from the heat and allow to cool slightly. Meanwhile, in a bowl, whisk together the remaining sugar and the flour. Whisk in the egg yolks

until well blended. Slowly pour about 125 ml (4 fl oz) of the hot milk into the egg mixture, stirring constantly. Pour the mixture back into the saucepan. Place over a low heat and cook, stirring constantly, for 5–10 minutes or until the custard is thick enough to coat the back of the spoon. Remove from the heat and pour through a fine-mesh sieve into a bowl. Stir in the vanilla extract and lemon zest. Leave to cool to room temperature, stirring occasionally to prevent a skin from forming.

4 Preheat the oven to 190°C (375°F). Pour the cooled custard into the pastry case and sprinkle the pine nuts evenly over the top. Place the flan tin on a baking tray and bake for about 35 minutes or until the top of the filling is just set and the pastry is golden brown. Transfer the tart, in the tin, to a wire rack and leave to cool completely. Remove the side of the tin and slide the tart off the base on to a flat serving plate. Serve at room temperature.

Serve with an Italian dessert wine, such as Moscato Passito di Pantelleria from Sicily or Muffato della Sala from Umbria.

FOR THE PASTRY DOUGH

90 g (3 oz) unsalted butter, at room temperature, cut into 6 pieces

75 g (2½ oz) icing sugar, sifted

1 tablespoon honey

Few drops of pure vanilla extract

½ teaspoon grated lemon zest

Pinch of salt

2 large egg yolks

220 g (7 oz) soft-wheat flour, sifted

½ teaspoon baking powder

FOR THE FILLING

500 ml (16 fl oz) whole milk

250 g (8 oz) granulated sugar

60 g (2 oz) plain flour

4 egg yolks

⅛ teaspoon pure vanilla extract

Grated zest of 1 lemon

45 g (1½ oz) pine nuts

Makes one 23–24-cm
(9–9½-inch) cake, or 8 servings

FONDENTE AL CIOCCOLATO

Rich Chocolate Cakes

While hardly a Roman tradition, a rich, dense chocolate cake is found on many of the city's dessert menus, including that of Ristorante Agata e Romeo, the inspiration for this recipe. It makes a superb showcase for Italian chocolate, whose purity was the subject of a debate that split the European Union in 2003, with France and Italy fighting to defend their superior products. Although the final ruling legalized the use of 5 per cent other vegetable fats (a practice previously banned in Italy), it also brought improved labelling, to help consumers. Amedei chocolate, from Tuscany, is a favourite of Roman foodies.

FOR THE CRÈME ANGLAISE

250 ml (8 fl oz) whole milk

1 vanilla pod, split lengthways, or ⅛ teaspoon pure vanilla extract

3 large egg yolks

90 g (3 oz) sugar

FOR THE CAKES

250 ml (8 fl oz) double cream

220 g (7 oz) dark plain chocolate, preferably 70 per cent cocoa solids, cut into small pieces

2 large egg yolks

2 tablespoons sugar

2 tablespoons plain flour, sifted

Cocoa powder for dusting

Makes 4 servings

1 To make the crème anglaise, in a heavy saucepan combine the milk and vanilla pod (if using vanilla extract, add it later). Set over a moderate heat and heat until small bubbles appear round the edge. Remove from the heat and allow to cool slightly. Meanwhile, in a bowl, whisk together the egg yolks and sugar for about 5 minutes or until thick and pale yellow. Slowly pour the hot milk into the egg mixture, stirring constantly. Pour the contents of the bowl back into the saucepan, place over a low heat, and cook gently, stirring constantly, for 5–10 minutes or until the custard is thick enough to coat the back of the spoon. Remove from the heat and remove and discard the vanilla pod. Pour the custard through a fine-mesh sieve into a bowl. Stir in the vanilla extract, if using. Leave to cool to room temperature, stirring occasionally to prevent a skin from forming.

2 Preheat the oven to 220°C (425°F). Generously butter four 175-ml (6-fl oz) individual cake tins or moulds, dust with flour, and tap out the excess.

3 To make the cakes, combine the cream and chocolate in a heatproof bowl set over (but not touching) barely simmering water, and heat, stirring occasionally, until the chocolate melts and the mixture is smooth and evenly blended. Remove from the heat and set aside to cool slightly.

4 In a bowl, using a whisk or a hand-held electric mixer, beat together the egg yolks and sugar for about 5 minutes or until thick and pale yellow. Pour in the chocolate mixture in a thin stream, whisking constantly. Gently whisk in the flour.

5 Divide the chocolate mixture evenly among the prepared tins. Arrange the tins on a baking tray. Bake for about 10 minutes or until the top of each cake is firm to the touch. The centre of each cake will still be liquid. Transfer the cakes, still in their tins, to a wire rack and allow to cool for 5 minutes.

6 To serve, invert a dessert plate over each warm cake and, holding the plate and tin firmly together, invert them, then lift off the tin. If the cakes stick, ease them out with the tip of a knife. Spoon some of the cooled crème anglaise in a pool alongside each cake. Using a fine-mesh sieve, dust each cake with a little cocoa powder. Serve at once, with the remaining crème anglaise in a jug.

Chocolate is a difficult match, but for a local wine try Rosathea, a Moscato rosa from Castel de Paolis.

PECORINO CON PERE E CONFETTURA DI FICHI

Pecorino Romano with Sliced Pears and Fig Jam

Mature cheeses with fresh fruit and interesting, usually sweet condiments, such as artisanal honeys and fruit preserves, are popular desserts in the city's best restaurants. In winter, pecorino romano might be matched with pears and an easy jam made from dried figs, while in summer it might sit alongside fresh figs so ripe they're bursting their seams. Figs have grown in and around Rome since ancient times, and today the season is split between the larger fruits of early summer and the small fruits (settembrini) of late summer.

1 To make the jam, preheat the oven to 150°C (300°F). Spread the nuts in a single layer on a small baking tray and roast, shaking the tray halfway through, for 10–15 minutes or until the nuts darken and smell deliciously nutty. Pour on to a plate to cool. (There is no need to remove the skins.)

2 In a small saucepan combine the figs and 125 ml (4 fl oz) water and bring to the boil. Remove from the heat and allow to stand for 5 minutes.

3 Put the nuts in a food processor and pulse twice. Add the figs and their liquid, the brandy, sugar, and lemon zest and juice and pulse until the figs are coarsely chopped. Taste and add more sugar if you would prefer the jam to be sweeter.

4 Using a short, sharp knife, stab the cheese wedge and break off a chunk. Your want to make 4 nice chunks this way. Divide them among individual plates.

5 If their skins are blemish free, there is no need to peel the pears. Halve one pear and core it, then thinly slice one of the halves lengthways, keeping the slices together. Fan the slices on a plate next to the cheese. Repeat with the other half and then with the remaining pears. Divide the fig jam evenly among the plates. Alternatively, place the cheese and a cheese knife on a board, fan the pear halves on a serving plate, put the jam in a small bowl, and let everyone help themselves.

Serve with a sweet late harvest Est! Est!! Est!!! or a Muffato della Sala from just across the border in Umbria.

FOR THE FIG JAM

2 tablespoons filberts or almonds

125 g (¼ lb) moist dried figs (about 5 figs), stalks trimmed and each fig cut into 4 or 5 pieces

2 tablespoons brandy

2 tablespoons sugar, or to taste

Grated zest and juice of ½ lemon

185-g (6-oz) wedge *pecorino romano*, matured for at least 5 months

2 ripe pears such as Bosc or Rocha

Makes 4 servings

Sheep's milk cheeses

The official animal of Rome is the she-wolf that nurtured the city's founder, Romulus, and his twin, Remus, but perhaps a more appropriate symbol would be *la pecora,* "the sheep". The boys grew up to be shepherds, and sheep have been grazing in or around Rome – urban sprawl permitting – ever since, with the result that the most typical local cheeses, including *pecorino romano* and *ricotta romana,* are made from sheep's milk.

The DOP regulation (page 81) for *pecorino romano* restricts its production to a zone that includes all of Lazio and Sardinia and the Grosseto province in southern Tuscany. The cheese must be made from whole milk from sheep raised in the zone, curdled with lamb rennet. It is matured for five months for a table cheese and at least eight months for a grating cheese and is considered an essential in *trippa alla romana* (tripe) and many pastas.

Ricotta romana is made from heated whey mixed with whole sheep's milk and heated again. The solids are then packed into conical baskets to drain. Mild and creamy, ricotta is great when fried (sweetened or not), on pasta, or in desserts.

PIZZA DI VISCIOLE ALLA ROMANA
Sour Cherry Tart

Visciole are small, sour cherries that grow near Rome, and any Roman lucky enough to have a friend with a tree looks forward to the early summer harvest. Most visciole, like their even sourer relative, amarene, go straight into the jam pot, and it is the fate of most jams to end up spread in a thick tart case. The use of the word pizza, rather than crostata, for this traditional Roman tart illustrates how the term was once applied to many kinds of cakes, breads, and pies. If you are short of time, you can use any good-quality jam – about 315 g (10 oz) – that contains pieces of fruit.

FOR THE CHERRY JAM

500 g (1 lb 2 oz) sour cherries, stoned

125 g (4½ oz) granulated sugar

Pinch of ground cinnamon

FOR THE PASTRY DOUGH

1 whole egg plus 2 egg yolks

185 g (6 oz) granulated sugar

Pinch of salt

125 g (4 oz) plus 2 tablespoons unsalted butter, at room temperature, cut into 6 pieces

375 g (12 oz) soft-wheat flour

FOR THE CRÈME PÂTISSIÈRE

250 ml (8 fl oz) whole milk

1 large strip lemon zest

1 vanilla pod, split lengthways

3 egg yolks

60 g (2 oz) granulated sugar

2 tablespoons cornflour

1 egg yolk, lightly beaten

Icing sugar, sifted

Makes one 28-cm (11-inch) tart, or 6–8 servings

1 To make the cherry jam, in a heavy saucepan combine the cherries, granulated sugar, and cinnamon. Set over a moderate heat and bring to a simmer, stirring constantly to dissolve the sugar, then cook, stirring frequently, for about 15 minutes or until the cherries are fully softened and wrinkled and the mixture has thickened. Remove from the heat and set aside. The jam will thicken further as it cools.

2 To make the pastry dough, in a bowl whisk together the whole egg and egg yolks, granulated sugar, and salt until well blended. Gradually whisk in the butter a piece at a time until all of it has been incorporated. Add the flour a little at a time, working it in quickly with your fingers until it is incorporated and the dough is smooth. Divide the dough into 2 pieces, one slightly larger than the other. Form each piece into a disc, wrap separately in cling film, and chill for at least 2 hours or up to 24 hours.

3 To make the crème pâtissière, in a heavy saucepan combine the milk, lemon zest, and vanilla pod. Set over a moderate heat and heat until small bubbles appear round the edge. Remove from the heat and cool slightly, then remove and discard the lemon zest and vanilla pod. Meanwhile, in a bowl whisk together the egg yolks, granulated sugar, and cornflour for about 5 minutes or until thick and pale yellow. Slowly pour the hot milk into the egg mixture, stirring constantly. Pour the contents of the bowl back into the saucepan, place over a low heat, and cook, stirring constantly, for 5–10 minutes or until the custard is thick enough to coat the spoon.

Remove from the heat. Allow to cool to room temperature, then place cling film directly on the surface of the crème pâtissière and chill for at least 30 minutes or up to 24 hours.

4 Preheat the oven to 180°C (350°F). Butter a 28-cm (11-inch) flan tin with a lift-out base, dust with flour, and tap out the excess. Remove the larger disc of pastry from the fridge and place in the prepared tin. Using your hands, pat it evenly over the bottom and about 2.5 cm (1 inch) up the sides. Patch as needed to create a smooth surface.

5 Spread the cooled crème pâtissière in the pastry case, then evenly dot the crème pâtissière with spoonfuls of the jam. Using the back of the spoon, gently spread the jam over the top, covering the crème pâtissière completely in an even layer.

6 On a lightly floured work surface, roll out the remaining disc of pastry into a 28-cm (11-inch) round. Using a pastry wheel or knife, cut the round into 10 strips each about 2 cm (¾ inch) wide. Lay 5 strips across the filling. Lay the remaining 5 strips at right angles to the first strips to create a lattice pattern. Cut off and discard any excess pastry.

7 Bake the tart for 40–45 minutes or until the pastry is golden brown. Transfer to a wire rack to cool completely. Dust with icing sugar before serving.

Brachetto d'Acqui, a sweet effervescent red from Piedmont, is the perfect match for cherries.

GLOSSARY

ABBACCHIO In Rome this term refers to a milk-fed baby lamb, less than two months old, as well as to young lamb in general. In local dishes, such as *abbacchio alla cacciatora* (page 139), lamb is always cooked through. The Italian word for lamb is *agnello*.

AL DENTE Literally meaning "to the tooth", this Italian phrase refers to pasta or rice that has been cooked until tender but is still firm at the centre, thus offering some resistance to the bite. Most Italian-manufactured dried pastas have fairly accurate timing directions on the packet, but in general packet timings can be too long.

ANCHOVIES Blended in a sauce or draped over pizza, tiny *acciughe*, or *alici*, appear widely in Italian cookery. Whole anchovies layered with salt have the best flavour of the preserved products. To prepare salted anchovies, rinse them gently under cold running water. If a less assertive flavour is wanted, soak for 10 minutes before proceeding. Scrape the skin of each anchovy away with the tip of a knife and cut away the dorsal fin. Press the anchovy open, flattening it carefully from head to tail end. Lift away the backbone, then cut the anchovy into 2 fillets. Rinse again, then dry on kitchen paper and use as directed in the recipe. Oil-packed anchovies come as fillets and do not need to be rinsed before using.

ARTICHOKES Artichokes (*carciofi*) are the signature vegetable of Rome, where they liven up the table in winter and spring. The city's market vendors and able cooks have perfected a pain-staking method of cutting the bulbs in a circular pattern so that only the parts that are edible remain (page 106). The most important use of artichokes is for *carciofi alla giudia* (page 53) and *carciofi alla romana* (page 159), but they also turn up in frittatas, pastas, and dishes such as *vignarola* (page 94).

AUBERGINE In Italian kitchens, aubergines, called *melanzane*, are grilled; rolled, stuffed with a filling, and baked; or used in pasta sauces. The most familiar variety is the globe-shaped aubergine, which is usually large, resembles a pear in shape, and has a thin, shiny skin that ranges from ivory to lavender to deep purple. In many markets you also find the long Italian aubergines, which are smaller than globe aubergines and which have a deep purple skin.

BALSAMIC VINEGAR *Aceto balsamico tradizionale*, or traditional balsamic vinegar, comes from the area around Reggio Emilia and Modena in Emilia-Romagna. It is made from cooked Trebbiano and Lambrusco grape must. To be considered DOP (*denominazione origine protetta*), it must be aged for at least 12 years in a series of barrels constructed of a variety of aromatic woods. The final product is slightly thick and syrupy, with a sweet, mellow taste, and is used sparingly as a condiment on finished dishes. It should never be cooked. Less expensive versions of balsamic vinegar of varying quality are widely available; they can be used in vinaigrettes, marinades, and a variety of other preparations. A white balsamic vinegar is also available.

BASIL A member of the mint family, this iconic Mediterranean herb adds a highly aromatic flavour to foods when it is used fresh. It is traditionally paired with tomatoes and is considered an essential ingredient in many classic Italian dishes and in preparations such as pesto sauce.

BAY LEAF Strong and spicy, the whole glossy leaves of the bay tree (*Laurus nobilis*) are indispensable in long-simmered savoury preparations, most especially *ragù*. The leaves are almost always sold dried (fresh leaves are more bitter) and should be removed from a dish before serving.

BREADCRUMBS Used to make crispy toppings for baked dishes or to lend body to fillings and stuffings, breadcrumbs should be made from a slightly stale coarse country loaf. Trim the loaf of its crusts, then process in a food processor to form crumbs. Spread out the crumbs on a baking sheet and dry in a preheated 165°C (325°F) oven for about 15 minutes. Leave to cool, then process again until the crumbs are fine. Continue baking, stirring once or twice, for a further 15 minutes or until the breadcrumbs are a pale golden colour.

BRESAOLA This salt-cured, air-dried beef is considered a speciality of the Valtellina, an Alpine valley in Lombardy. It is usually served thinly sliced like prosciutto. It tastes less salty than prosciutto, however, and its texture is firmer. Often paired with rocket and shaved Parmesan, *bresaola* is served as both an *antipasto* and a light *secondo*.

BROAD BEANS Ranging in colour from white or pale green to brown, broad beans have a slightly bitter flavour. At the beginning of their season in spring, when the beans are at their most tender, you can simply slip them from their large pods and serve them raw with *pecorino romano*. If the beans are older or larger, they usually need to be skinned (though this is not done in Rome): quickly blanch them, then slip them out of their light green skins. Fresh and dried broad beans are very different and should not be substituted for each other in recipes.

BROCCOLETTI Although it is a relative of *cime di rape* (turnip tops), and tastes very similar, broccoletti (sprouting broccoli) differs slightly in appearance – at the ends of its leafy green stalks are clusters of broccoli-like florets. Be sure to remove any of the tough stalks and wilted leaves before cooking. If the skin on the lower part of the stalks is fibrous, peel it with a vegetable peeler. Sautéed with garlic and chilli, broccoletti makes a terrific side dish.

CAPERS The preserved, unopened flower buds of a wild shrub, *capperi* have a piquant flavour enjoyed throughout the Mediterranean. Unlike brined capers, those packed in sea salt retain their intense floral flavour and firm texture. Capers labelled "nonpareil" are smaller than the distinctly large capers sold in Italian markets. Rinse both salted and brined capers before using.

CHICK-PEAS Known in Italy as *ceci*, these round beige beans have a rich, nutty flavour and a firm texture. Because they hold their shape well during cooking, they are often used in hearty soups. Dried chick-peas must be soaked before cooking. Canned chick-peas are a convenient alternative; drain and rinse them well before use.

CHILLIES In Italy, small, fiery red chillies are known as *peperoncini*. Roman cooks add the whole chillies to everything from pasta sauce to sautéed vegetables, removing them before serving. (For milder heat, remove the seeds from the chillies before using.) *Peperoncini* can be found in Italian delicatessens and some supermarkets, but any small, dried red chilli will work as a substitute. Alternatively, you can substitute $\frac{1}{2}$ teaspoon dried chilli flakes for the *peperoncino*.

COURGETTES In general, small courgettes (*zucchine* in Italian) are preferred for their few seeds and full flavour, and are often sold with their flowers still attached as an indication of freshness. The versatile vegetables are cut into chunks, strips, or rounds, and deep-fried, sautéed, steamed, stewed, marinated, stuffed, grilled, or baked. The flowers are also eaten, usually stuffed and deep-fried.

DEEP-FRYING When done properly, deep-frying will yield light, tender seafood and vegetables. Maintaining a consistent high temperature causes the water naturally present in foods to convert to steam, which forces out any oil that might otherwise seep inside. A deep-frying thermometer is recommended for regulating the temperature. Adding foods to the hot oil in small batches will prevent large drops in temperature and ensure that foods are evenly submerged in the oil. In Italy extra virgin olive oil is typically used for both deep and shallow frying.

DRIED CHILLI FLAKES Flakes and seeds of *peperoncini,* slender dried red chillies, are a popular kitchen seasoning and table condiment in central and southern Italy. Just a pinch can add heat to many dishes. The chillies may be bottled already crushed or may be bought whole and crushed in a polythene bag with a rolling pin. When sautéing with dried chilli flakes, take care not to let them burn. See also Chillies.

FENNEL Sweet or Florence fennel, native to the Mediterranean region, is a vegetable valued for its green-white bulb and feathery fronds. Fennel is at its best in winter, when the bulb adds its crisp texture and faintly sweet liquorice flavour to salads. In Italy raw fennel (*finocchio*) is often paired with oranges or other citrus fruits. The bulbs can also be grilled or baked with Parmesan. To use cut off the long hollow stalks and any discoloured areas from the bulb, saving the feathery fronds to snip with scissors or to use whole as a garnish.

FIGS The ancient Romans believed figs, or *fichi,* imported from Greece were superior to those grown on local trees. Italians today are happy with their own harvests, eating them with prosciutto between slices of *pizza bianca*, baking them into breads, or mixing them with nuts and honey for *biscotti*. Figs seem to flourish everywhere in Italy. They are cultivated in gardens and also grow wild, pushing

their way through crevices in stone walls and ancient parapets. Many varieties ripen twice a year. In Rome the small, sweet green or black figs of early autumn are called *settembrini* (little Septembers).

GUANCIALE See page 101.

HAZELNUTS Called *nocciole* in Italian, these nuts grow in abundance in northern Lazio and find their way into everything from biscotti to gelato. Grape-sized hazelnuts have hard shells that come to a point like an acorn, cream-coloured flesh, and a sweet, rich, buttery flavour. They usually are sold already shelled.

MARJORAM The delicate floral flavour of marjoram blends beautifully with the other ingredients in many Italian recipes, especially when partnered with tomatoes. It has a milder flavour than oregano, a close cousin. Marjoram is best when used fresh.

MASCARPONE Very rich and ultra-smooth mascarpone is used in cooking as well as being essential for many popular Italian desserts, most notably *tiramisù*. Although it is considered a cheese, mascarpone is really a thickened cream.

OLIVE OIL See page 81.

ONIONS, SWEET A variety of Italian onion that has recently gained popularity outside of Italy is the red *cipolla di Tropea*, named for a seaside town in Calabria. Medium sized and shaped like a top, these sweet onions are almost always eaten fresh rather than cooked. Vidalia or another sweet variety of onion can be substituted.

OXTAIL Oxtail, called *coda di bue* in Italian, has never gone out of fashion as traditional comfort food. Long, slow cooking mellows the meat and releases the gelatine from the bones, making a wonderfully rich and savoury braise or stew.

PANCETTA See page 101.

PARSLEY, FLAT-LEAF This variety of the popular Mediterranean herb, called *prezzemolo* in Italian, has a more complex, peppery flavour than the curly-leaf type, which is rarely seen in Italy.

PASTA See page 36.

PASSATA Available in bottles and cartons, passata is simply tomatoes that have been puréed and then sieved to remove all the bits of skin and seeds.

PEPPERS Sweet-fleshed peppers (*peperoni*), be they bell-shaped or long and slim, are all members of the Capsicum family. Green peppers are usually more sharply flavoured than red ones, the latter being simply a sweeter and more mature stage of the former. Orange and yellow peppers are separate varieties. Peppers travelled to Italy after Columbus's voyages to America and were at first cultivated for decorative purposes only, their edibility being regarded with great suspicion.

PINE NUTS These long, slender nuts, the seeds of umbrella-shaped stone pines that grow throughout the Mediterranean, are high in oil and have a delicate flavour. Called *pinoli* in Rome and *pignoli* in some other parts of Italy, pine nuts are used in both savoury and sweet recipes. The nuts are sprinkled on pasta or added to meat sauces, and are used with fresh basil and olive oil to make *pesto alla genovese*. They are also an ingredient in some tarts and cakes, such as *Torta della Nonna* (page 177).

PIZZA PEEL Cooks, especially professional bakers, place pizzas on this large, flat wooden tool so they can be transferred to and from the oven safely and with ease. Peels measure 60 cm (24 inches) or more in diameter and have a thin edge and long handle. A flat, sturdy baking sheet can be used for the same purpose.

PIZZA STONE Also called a baking stone or baking tile, this square, rectangular, or round slab of unglazed stoneware creates the effect of a brick oven in a domestic oven. The stone should be preheated in the oven for at least 45 minutes or up to 1 hour before baking. The pizza or other bread is slid on to the hot stone using a pizza peel.

POTATOES The common Italian variety of potato for boiling has a waxy, yellow flesh. Charlotte and Roseval are good substitutes.

PROSCIUTTO Prosciutto is made from the hind thigh of a pig just under a year old, and is cured at length under special conditions. Delicately flavoured *prosciutto di Parma*, from the Emila-Romagna region, comes from pigs fed, among other things, whey left over from the process of making the area's

Parmigiano-Reggiano (Parmesan). *Prosciutto di San Daniele,* from Friuli in north-eastern Italy, is pressed into a distinctive violin-like shape, while Parma *prosciutti* are rounder. Both have dense, red meat and creamy white fat. *Prosciutto di montagna* is a more generic term used in Rome to describe a less expensive, saltier, and more rustic style of prosciutto.

PUNTARELLE See page 45.

ROSEMARY Taking its name from the Latin for "dew of the sea", reflecting its relationship to ocean-side climates, this herb is native to the Mediterranean and contributes a powerful but pleasantly aromatic flavour to lamb, veal, chicken, and a host of other foods. It is, without a doubt, the most popular herb in Roman cooking.

SAGE An ancient healing herb that takes its name from the Latin *salvus,* meaning "safe", this heady, slightly musty-tasting herb (called *salvia* in Italian) is usually used fresh in Italian dishes. It is an essential ingredient in the dish *Saltimbocca alla Romana* (page 127).

SALT COD *Baccalà,* salt cod, is a fixture on Friday menus throughout Rome, in keeping with *il venerdi di magro,* the Catholic church's tradition of meatless Friday, which has become as much a gastronomic as a religious observance. The prevalence of salt cod in Italy harks back to the time when lack of refrigeration or rapid transport made access to fresh fish in inland cities nearly impossible. In the fifteenth century, whalers off the coast of Newfoundland learned to preserve precious Atlantic cod (*merluzzo* in Italian) by salting it. They cleaned and salted the cod on board the fishing boats, then dried it on land.

SAMBUCA This anise-flavoured Roman liqueur can be enjoyed as a shot in coffee for *caffè corretto,* an after-dinner drink, or as a flavouring in desserts such as *zuppa inglese.* It is sometimes offered *con le mosche* (with flies), with two coffee beans floating freely in the glass.

SCAMORZA Pear-shaped, with a firm yet springy and elastic texture, this is a *pasta filata* cheese very similar to mozzarella. It may be made from cow's or sheep's milk or a mixture of the two. Its flavour is mild and slightly salty. Like mozzarella, scamorza is sometimes smoked (*affumicate*).

SEMOLINA This somewhat coarse flour is milled from durum wheat, a variety that is particularly high in protein. The flour is almost always used in the manufacture of dried pastas. It is also used in some pizza doughs and breads.

SPAGHETTI FORK A spaghetti fork is a handy instrument with a long handle and a round, concave head with stubby prongs and a hole in the middle. It is perfect for stirring strand pasta such as spaghetti or retrieving it from the water once it is cooked.

TOMATOES See page 151.

INGREDIENT SOURCES

A.G. FERRARI FOODS
Olive oil, pasta, cured meats, pecorino and other cheeses.

www.agferrari.com

DI BRUNO BROTHERS
Will ship fine olive oils, pastas, some sheep's milk cheeses, and coffee from Illy, Kimbo, and Lavazza.

www.dibruno.com

DITALIA
Source for mature *pecorino romano,* balsamic vinegar, Kimbo coffee, and more.

www.ditalia.com

GUSTIAMO
A fine source for Italian pasta, rice, sweets, and even some Sabine olive oils.

www.gustiamo.com

MANGIBENE
A range of cured meats, including *bresaola,* plus artisanal pastas, cheeses, and chocolates.
+39 045 634 8757
www.mangibene.it

NASO E GOLA
Prosciutto di Parma, balsamic vinegar, Amadei chocolate, and more.

www.nasoegola.com

PAOLINO'S GOURMET ITALIAN FOOD
Sells artisanal pasta, including Latini brand, as well as extra virgin olive oils.

www.gourmetitalianfood.com

INDEX

A

Abbacchio, 185

Al dente, 185

Aleatico di Gradoli, 57

Anchovies
  dressing, *puntarelle* with, 160
  fried courgette flowers with mozzarella and, 77
  pizza with roasted sweet peppers, tomatoes, and, 121
  preparing salted, 185

Artichokes
  about, 185
  braised whole, 159
  carciofi alla giudia, 52–53
  fusilli with, 106
  stewed spring vegetables, 94
  varieties of, 52

Asparagus frittata, 82

Aubergine
  about, 185
  grilled, sweet peppers and, 70

B

Balsamic vinegar, 185

Bars, 17, 32, 34

Basil
  about, 127, 185
  garlic-rubbed toast with fresh tomatoes and, 69
  pasta shells with mozzarella, tomatoes, and, 105

Bay leaves, 185

Beans. *See also* Broad beans; Chick-peas
  romano, with tomatoes, 163
  varieties of, 163

Béchamel sauce, 117

Beef. *See also Bresaola*; Oxtail
  fettuccine with meat sauce, 113
  rice croquettes, 73
  sautéed strips of, with rocket, 135

Biscotti, hazelnut, 173

Bread
  about, 69
  crumbs, 185
  garlic-rubbed toast with fresh tomatoes and basil, 69

Bresaola
  about, 185
  with rocket and Parmesan, 81

Broad beans
  about, 163, 185
  stewed spring vegetables, 94

Broccoletti, 45
  about, 185
  with garlic and chilli, 152

Broccolo romanesco
  about, 44
  pasta with, 102

Bruschetta, 69

Bucatini, 40

C

Cafés, 34

Cakes
  rich chocolate, 178
  sponge, with custard and liqueur, 174

Campo de' Fiori, 21–22, 26

Cannoli, 62

Capers, 185

Cappelletti, 40

Carciofi alla giudia, 52–53

Castagnaccio, 62

Cerveteri, 56

Cesanese, 57

Cheese
  Gorgonzola, potato gnocchi with radicchio and, 118
  mozzarella, fried courgette flowers with anchovies and, 77
  mozzarella, pasta shells with tomatoes, basil, and, 105
  mozzarella di bufala, 105
  onion and herb tart, 86
  pecorino, tonnarelli with pepper and, 109
  pecorino romano with sliced pears and fig jam, 181
  pizza with roasted sweet peppers, tomatoes, and anchovies, 121
  rice croquettes, 73
  ricotta mousse, strawberries with, 169
  ricotta tart, 170

sheep's milk, 181
  spaghetti with eggs, cured pork, and, 98

Cherry tart, sour, 182

Chicken
  breasts, pan-fried, with herbs, 131
  with tomatoes and sweet peppers, 144

Chick-peas
  about, 185
  and pasta soup, 93

Chicory, wild *(cicoria selvatica)*, 44

Chillies, 185
  dried chilli flakes, 186

Chocolate
  cakes, rich, 178
  ricotta tart, 170

Ciambelline, 60–61, 63

Clams in their shells, spaghetti with, 110

Coffee, 32. *See also* Bars

Cornetto, 62

Courgettes
  about, 186
  flowers, fried, with mozzarella and anchovies, 77
  slices, marinated, 74
  stuffed, 140

Crème anglaise, 178

Croquettes, rice, 73

Crostata di frutta, 63

Cucina ebraica, 50

Cuisine, Roman
  contemporary, 13–14, 17–18
  history of, 11–12, 155

D

Deep-frying, 185

Diavoletti al peperoncino, 63

Dolci
  ancient Roman, 61
  recipes for, 61, 169–82
  religious occasions and, 58
  varieties of, 58, 62–63, 167

E

Eggs
  asparagus frittata, 82
  spaghetti with cured pork, cheese, and, 98

ACKNOWLEDGMENTS

Maureen B Fant would like to thank, in particular, Mina Botti, Iris Carulli, Charlotte Cox, and Fanny Farkas for their invaluable help. Marinella Ercoli, Judith Harris, Howard Isaacs, Armando Manni, Maria Persia, Francesco Retacchi, Gwen and Franco Romagnoli, Bonnie Shershow, and Susan Wolf also provided assistance. A number of restaurateurs and chefs of Rome unselfishly shared recipes and advice: Sebastiano Allegrini, Enrico Licata and Franco Bartolini, Agata Parisella and Romeo Caraccio, Eugenio De Santis, Dario and Iole Cappellanti, Elio and Francesco Mariani, and Angelo and Massimo Troiani. In a class by herself is Oretta Zanini De Vita, walking encyclopaedia of Italian food history and generous friend. Finally, there is Francesco Filippi – Franco – whose companionship, intelligence, and appetite were priceless stimuli at every stage.

Weldon Owen and the photography team, including Jean-Blaise Hall and George Dolese, wish to thank Elisa Zucchiatti for her incredible help and guidance, and Maureen Fant for going out of her way to lend a hand in Rome. They would also like to extend their gratitude to the owners and workers of restaurants, bakeries, shops, and other culinary businesses in Rome who participated in this project: Patrizia Mattei and the others at Antico Arco, Vittorio Procaccia at Vini e Buffet, Susy Porcelli and family at Checco er Carettiere, Claudio Ceccarelli at Hostaria Giggetto, Luciano Flamini at Maccherone, and the people at Al Vino Al Vino and Pizzeria Gaudi. A big thank you to Elizabeth and the staff at C.U.C.I.N.A for supplying us with a beautiful selection of tablewares. Jean-Blaise Hall in particular would like to thank his assistant Sandra Mahut for her great spirits on this project, as well as Trattoria Frontoni, Ristorante Paris, Pierluigi Roscioli and family at Roscioli, Casa Bleve, Pasticceria Vitti, Ristorante Il Convivio, Gelateria Giolitti, Checchino dal 1887, Antica Caciara, Panella bakery, fresh pasta shops Pasta Al'Uovo and Grand Gourmet, Hosteria Romana, Pasticceria Valzani, gourmet food shop Castroni, E. Volpetti & Co., Drogheria Innocenzi, Pizzeria Ai Marmi, Ristorante Agata e Romeo, Enoteca Cavour 313, Il Gelato di San Crispino, Dar Filettaro a Santa Barbara, Bar S. Eustachio, Tazza d'Oro, Gelateria Bar Sisto, La Rotonda, Ristorante Al Presidente, La Bottega del Cioccolato, 'Gusto, Ristorante La Rosetta, Enoteca Al Parlamento, butcher Angelo Feroa, the Antico Forno bakery, La Campannina restaurant in Ostia, and Trattoria Bucci in Castel Gandolfo. The team would also like to thank Susan and Joseph Miller for their generous hospitality and assistance, as well as Spark restaurant in Los Angeles and Oliveto and Citron restaurants in Oakland, California.

Weldon Owen wishes to thank the following individuals for their kind assistance: Desne Ahlers, Cecilia Brunazzi, Ken DellaPenta, Judith Dunham, Arin Hailey, Lesli Neilson, Joan Olson, Stephanie Rosenbaum, Sharon Silva, and Paolo Sortino.

PHOTO CREDITS
Jean-Blaise Hall: All photography, except for the following:
Paul Moore: Pages 56–57
©Gustavo Tomsich/CORBIS: Page 155

PHOTOGRAPHY LOCATIONS

The following locations have been given map references for the map on pages 28–29.

BONNIER BOOKS

Appledram Barns

Birdham Road

Chichester, West Sussex

PO20 7EQ

FOODS OF THE WORLD ROME

Originally published as

Williams-Sonoma Foods of the World Rome

Conceived and produced by Weldon Owen Inc.

814 Montgomery Street, San Francisco, CA 94133

Telephone: 415-291-0100 Fax: 415-291-8841

In Collaboration with Williams-Sonoma, Inc.

3250 Van Ness Avenue, San Francisco, CA 94109

A Weldon Owen Production

First printed in 2005

10 9 8 7 6 5 4 3 2 1

ISBN 978-1905825-10-3

Printed by Tien Wah Press

Printed in Singapore

WELDON OWEN INC.

Chief Executive Officer John Owen

President and Chief Operating Officer Terry Newell

Vice President International Sales Stuart Laurence

Vice President and Creative Director Gaye Allen

Vice President and Publisher Hannah Rahill

Series Editor Kim Goodfriend

Project Editor Emily Miller

Editorial Assistant Juli Vendzules

Art Director Nicky Collings

Designers Alison Fenton, Rachel Lopez

Production Director Chris Hemesath

Color Manager Teri Bell

Production and Shipping Coordinator Todd Rechner

Food Stylist George Dolese

Associate Food Stylist Elisabet der Nederlanden

Prop Stylists George Dolese and Maggie Ward

Photographer's Assistants Sandra Mahut,

Jeremy Michael Weiss, Brooke Buchanan

Map Illustrator Bart Wright

Translator Norma MacMillan